Paul Duncan

The Pocket Essential

ALFRED HITCHCOCK

First published in Great Britain 1999. This updated edition published 2002 by
Pocket Essentials, 18 Coleswood Road, Harpenden, Herts, AL5 1EQ

Distributed in the USA by Trafalgar Square Publishing,
PO Box 257, Howe Hill Road, North Pomfret, Vermont 05053

A CIP catalogue record for this book is available from the British Library.

ISBN 1-903047-00-5

2 4 6 8 10 9 7 5 3

Book typeset by Pdunk
Printed and bound by Cox & Wyman

for Claude and Josef

Acknowledgements

For their help filling gaps in my video, book and clippings collection, and for ideas, I would like to thank John Ashbrook, Colin Odell, Michelle LeBlanc, Ellen Cheshire and John Kennedy Melling. For his encouragement, thanks to Hitchcock admirer Ed Gorman. For inspiring me, thanks to Claude and Josef.

CONTENTS

Alfred Hitchcock: Inspiring Public Unease

I had a dream once. I'm at LAX (Los Angeles airport) and I'm waiting for my case to slide down the chute. There are lots and lots of people milling about. They are nondescript. I see my case on the carousel, pick it up and roll it towards Customs. I've got drink to declare but, before I get there, I trip on my laces. A Customs man walks towards me, asks if everything is okay. I'm fine. I crouch to tie my laces. He picks up my case and dusts it off. As he does so, I look at my case and realise it is not mine. My heart misses a beat.

Looking at my face, the Customs man realises something's wrong. He asks me to accompany him to his desk. I pause, then get up. Slowly, I walk towards his table, watching him unlock the case, open it. I can only see his eyes look down, then look up at me. "Is this your case, sir?" he asks me. I wake up in dread. What was in that case? I knew it was something bad.

Alfred Hitchcock pervades our consciousness. There is no doubt in my mind that virtually everyone in the Western world has seen at least one of his movies. We have seen the world through his eyes and we find it frightening. Alfred Hitchcock was afraid, and he was able to communicate his fear through the use of situation.

His films are scary, not because the people are scary, but because they are nice, even attractive. Awkward, shy, gawky Norman Bates - he wouldn't hurt a fly.

His films are scary, not because they take place in the dark shadows of the night, but because they are situated in bright sunlight, in plain sight, amongst the crowd.

His films are scary, not because he is explicit or direct, but because his world-view is coded in abstraction. *The Birds* ends with the world in chaos. Mankind has to tiptoe through the rest of their lives because, at any moment, the world will turn on them. In *Vertigo* an obsessed man sees the woman he loves killed twice - life not only puts the knife in, it twists it as well.

The reason why people are uneasy about watching Hitchcock is because they know he is capable of killing his characters. He knows that their experiences in the story may damage or cripple them forever. Janet Leigh is killed in *Psycho*. Mrs Thorwald is killed and chopped up in *Rear Window*. Vera Miles ends up in a sanatorium at the end of *The Wrong Man*. People are killed in virtually every movie he made. Worse than that,

Hitchcock shows you the killing and the killers but you do not avert your eyes - you want to see it all.

Hitchcock is not Hitchcockian. When people describe a Brian De Palma or Richard Franklin or whoever film as being Hitchcockian they are usually referring to certain camera movements and angles. They refer to the visual language that Hitchcock used. People are then confused when they see Hitchcock's movies, because they are never quite the same as the modern movies. The reason for this is because Hitchcock's visual language is developed from story, and the story is one of suspense.

Suspense is the art of telling you that something bad is going to happen in a specific time-frame, but you do not want the bad thing to happen. This tension is held by Hitchcock, who strings you along and plays you like a fiddle. His most ambitious, sustained and, it must be said, successful attempt was *Psycho* - after Janet Leigh is killed we are not let off the hook until the end of the film, over an hour later. However, the Hitchcockian directors mostly concentrate on the shock aspects of *Psycho* rather than the suspense elements.

After looking at quite a few films, I began to develop a view of Hitchcock as a cubist film-maker. What I mean by this is that he places the characters within an imaginary cube and moves the camera along the sides of the cube. This gives his films a uniquely formal quality. Think of the following angles:

When seen from the back, we are discovering/seeing the world from the protagonist's point of view.

When seen from the front, we are seeing the protagonist's reaction to the world they are seeing.

When seen from above, we are seeing the ironical, detached point of view, without emotion.

When seen from the side, we are seeing someone else's point of view of the character, usually sinister because there is no eye contact. Then the character turns to look at us and we are afraid of them. This is used to great effect in *Shadow Of A Doubt* when Joseph Cotten is at the dinner table talking about strangling rich widows, Teresa Wright looking at him, seeing the side of his face.

Control

Hitchcock controlled his life with obsessive detail. He never liked to leave his office during working hours. He wore the same type of suit and tie so that he didn't have to think about clothes. He took the same suites in hotels around the world, so that he knew where he was, felt comfortable, safe.

He controlled his films in the same way. Trained as an artist, he drew the film before filming. Film is a visual medium after all. Just as an artist collects fruits or models to paint, Hitchcock collected actors. Does an artist depict the feelings of the model, or does the artist project the sympathetic part of themselves upon the model? I think the latter is the case.

To Hitchcock, actors represented a style of person, in the way that buildings represented a style of architecture. A balanced and directed combination of elements results in a whole vision. To Hitchcock, the actors were part of both the image, the story and the subtext.

Although critics tend to lump the James Stewart films together, or the Cary Grant films, and imply obsessions with actors and actresses, they forget to tell you that Hitchcock constantly switched from one actor to another as the style and content of the stories dictated. James Stewart appeared in films in 1948, 1954, 1956 and 1958. Cary Grant appeared in films in 1941, 1946, 1955 and 1959. This is not obsessive behaviour from a man who made 21 films between 1941 and 1959.

All the evidence seems to point to Hitchcock being obsessed with the main female protagonists in his films. The theory of many critics who analyse his work is that on screen Hitch liked to perform sadistic acts on his actresses, yet many of the actresses themselves (except Tippi Hedren) said that Hitch was a perfect gentleman, sometimes over-protective, and almost fatherly in his concern. Whatever the truth, it has to be said that most of his films feature very strong female leads or, at least, the stories are about troubled women. *Blackmail* (1929) is about what we now call date rape, where the woman kills the man who attacks her. The blackmailer gets killed and the woman walks off scot-free. There are many Hitchcock films from a female perspective: *Sabotage, Rebecca, Spellbound, Suspicion, Shadow Of A Doubt, Marnie*... And the female characters in the others are more than a match for any man. In his films, women are independent, opinionated, qualified and often quite aware of their sexuality.

Experimentation

It is something of an understatement to say that Hitchcock was an accomplished storyteller. One can see that after, say, twenty films or so, it could get boring unless you stretched yourself every now and again. Hitchcock stretched himself with some amazingly minimalist films. *Lifeboat* was a film about a group of people in a lifeboat. That's it. That's all the production designer had to do - a few bits of wreckage, the odd hull, a sky, some choppy water and he's sorted. *Rope* is a series of eight 10-minute takes in one apartment room. *Rear Window* is about James Stewart, in a wheelchair, leg in plaster, in a room, watching and listening to people in and around a courtyard.

Hitchcock was constantly striving to tell stories in as imaginative a way as possible. The phenomenal number of visual ideas he had in his work, especially in his early films, were heavily influenced by the German Expressionistic films of the 1920s, which used trick photography and symbolic images to tell stories. As his style and confidence grew, Hitchcock abandoned the symbolic images, and only used trick photography and special editing techniques for key moments in his films. Another reason for this is because, with the introduction of sound and music, a lot more fact and emotion could be conveyed without the need for visual symbolism.

Also, the occasional camera movement in the early films is noticeable because the rest of the films were static. By, for example, *Suspicion* (1941) Hitchcock had wholly integrated camera movement into his style and the camera was flying about all over the place. The movement, I hasten to add, is not gratuitous but completely serves the telling of the story.

Story

Much is made of Hitchcock's acute visual sense, and the spectacular set pieces he concocted. Yet, they had to have plot, and they must have characters, although the measure of each varied depending on the type of film Hitchcock made.

The best writers in the world wrote for Hitchcock: Dorothy Parker, Ben Hecht, Raymond Chandler, John Steinbeck, Thornton Wilder, Evan Hunter, Brian Moore.

Although not bad, the source material was never brilliant. It is significant that Hitchcock never adapted a literary masterpiece to the screen. This was because he believed, quite rightly, that if a genuine masterpiece had found its definitive form as a book, Hitch couldn't improve on it. Hitchcock only adapted those stories which lent themselves to visual interpretation. Furthermore, he had no hesitation in completely jettisoning scenes and characters from his source material in order to serve the film. Raymond Chandler, when working on the script for *Strangers On A Train*, complained that Hitchcock had already completely visualised the film in his head, so Chandler couldn't add anything but dialogue to progress the film from one visual to another.

It is not generally known that Hitchcock's greatest collaborator was his wife, Alma. One day older, she had begun work in movies at the age of 16, working her way up to the post of continuity girl and editor a long time before Hitchcock had doodled his first title for the silents. She was credited on many of his films, from Hitchcock's first in 1925 up until *Stage Fright* in 1950, but she had far more of an impact than those credits suggest. Alma had a sharp brain and she wasn't afraid to use it. Each day, when Hitchcock returned home, he would discuss the day's script with her and together they would tighten it, then come up with new visual and verbal ideas for the next day's session with whichever world-famous writer he was currently employing. His collaborators often complained (to biographers) that Alma's name was on the credits, citing Hitchcock's predilection for extra cash as the reason for Alma's credit, but they missed the point entirely - she was an unseen part of the team.

For Hitchcock, the film was a continuous series of images which resulted in a physical and/or emotional response. His roller-coaster ride of *The Man Who Knew Too Much* is repeated in *The 39 Steps*, *Young And Innocent*, *Foreign Correspondent*, *Saboteur*, etc. right up until *North By Northwest*. He left the field open for action heroes from James Bond to Arnold Schwarzenegger to exploit.

He rearranged the plot to set up either surprise or suspense situations - mostly he selected suspense. The novel *The Living And The Dead* by Boileau & Narcejac, the basis for Hitchcock's movie *Vertigo*, tells two stories concurrently, one in flashback, which reveals in its closing passages that the woman in both stories is one and the same. That is a surprise saved for the end. Hitchcock rearranged the structure, telling one story after the other, so that the first story is about the dead woman and the second is about the living. Early on in the second story, he reveals to the audience, but not to James Stewart's character, that the woman is one and the same. This has two effects. Firstly, the woman and her motives become real and understandable. Secondly, we are held in suspense for an hour, waiting for James Stewart to find out the secret, and wondering what he'll do next.

It should be recognised that Hitchcock did more than one type of film. People talk as though they are all the same, as though they were supposed to elicit the same emotions from people all the time. This is blatantly untrue, although it is true to say he did make similar films, as the following list makes clear: Man On The Run (*The 39 Steps*, *Saboteur*, *North By Northwest*); Spy Thriller (*Secret Agent*, *Notorious*, *Torn Curtain*, *Topaz*); Horror Suspense (*The Lodger*, *Blackmail*, *Psycho*, *The Birds*); The Wrong Man (*The Wrong Man*, *I Confess*, *Frenzy*); Psychological (*Spellbound*, *Strangers On A Train*, *Vertigo*, *Marnie*); Murder Mystery (*Murder!*, *Dial M For Murder*, *Rear Window*); and Black Comedy (*The Trouble With Harry*, *Family Plot*).

The problem with doing such a list, of course, is that everyone is going to disagree about placing the films in a certain category. I sympathise, because many of Hitchcock's films can be placed in several categories, depending on your point of view. For example, *Frenzy* lurks somewhere between horror suspense, the wrong man, the man on the run and black comedy, depending upon whether your point of view is the killer, the man accused of the killing or the policeman investigating the case.

Horror

Suspense is the feeling of being afraid for one or more characters in the movie. Ooh-err, that boy is going to get blown up in *Sabotage*. Goodness, Teresa Wright is going to get murdered by Uncle Joe Cotten in *Shadow Of A Doubt*.

Horror is being afraid for yourself as much as for other people. In film, the horror moments are often triggered by surprise or by images which are unacceptable to society. Horror films are great fun, they give you a fright, you release lots of pent-up emotions and then you forget them. These films show a distorted reality using light and sound, but they always return to reality in the end. Horror tales are moral tales - they are adult versions of children's fairy tales. Far from being disruptive and a bad influence, they reinforce a white, Christian view of the world.

Hitchcock marked a change of approach to the suspense thriller film, by turning it into a horror thriller film. He did this with *Psycho*, financially his most successful film. Significantly, it was made as a cheap little experiment by Hitchcock's TV crew, not his usual film crew. It is also much more like his TV series, the *Roald Dahl's Tales Of The Unexpected*, sting-in-the-tail type of stories. The texture of the film is grainy, realistic, almost documentary, like *The Wrong Man*, as opposed to the smooth, luxurious images of his big-budget films.

The surprising and unacceptable images? Well, showing people in vests/underwear, sweating, going to the toilet, Janet Leigh getting killed off a half hour into the movie. Take your pick.

From very early on in his career, Hitch put the viewer in the position of his characters. You see a character on the screen looking at something, you see what they see (you in their position), then you see the character react to that something. It's simple.

In *The Lodger*, the Bunting family look up at their ceiling to see the light fittings shake, then we are looking up at the ceiling, at the light fittings shaking, the ceiling made of glass and watching the lodger walking up and down. That's in 1927.

In *Rear Window*, we are in the position of James Stewart, realising something is wrong, but not being able to do anything about it, being helpless in the wheelchair, as we are helpless in our cinema seats.

In *Psycho*, we are Norman Bates, looking through a hole in the wall, at Janet Leigh undressing (the beautiful, forbidden, pure Janet Leigh). In this film, more than any other, we are both the villain and the hero, able to switch sides, to satisfy both our civilised and uncouth instincts.

Glass Half Empty

Ultimately, Hitchcock's world-view was more pessimistic than optimistic. His films give a satisfying physical resolution (the baddie dies, the accused man does not get put in jail) but the mental anguish and consequences continue (the mastermind is still at large, the central character has to live with their mistakes, people are dead). Fry falls off The Statue Of Liberty at the end of *Saboteur*, yet the upper-class mastermind and his associates remain free to plot against the US Government. At the end of *Blackmail*, the girl and her detective boyfriend walk off into the distance, but they do not embrace, hold hands or show any affection or connection. Their trust in each other has gone, and may never be repaired. The same can be said of Cary Grant and Joan Fontaine at the end of *Suspicion*.

This is why Hitchcock's films will survive, because they give food for thought. They unsettle us and we don't know why. They do not assume we are morons. They let us work things out for ourselves. Eventually, we work out that Hitchcock is telling us that there are no pat solutions to life, that things don't necessarily work out right in the end.

I am at the Greyhound bus station in San Diego, reading a magazine. I'm engrossed in an article. I glance at my watch and, shit, I'm late. I run towards my stop. I'm knocking people aside, people looking at me, shouting, angry. I bump hard, straight on, into a middle-aged man. He falls back, hits his head on the tiled floor. People stop. stare, surround. They look down at the man and see two roses of blood, one around his head and the other on his stomach - he's been stabbed. They look up to my hands, my red hands. They accuse me. They surround me.

I don't wake up.

I'm not dreaming.

It's not a movie.

1. Silent Hitchcock (1922-1929)

Born in Leytonstone, a suburb of London, on 13 August 1899, Alfred Joseph Hitchcock was the son of a poulterer and greengrocer. The former trade gave Hitchcock a lifelong disgust of eggs (which is why the characters in his films treat eggs so badly - for example, in *To Catch A Thief*, Jessie stubs her cigarette in the yoke of an egg), and the latter gave him a taste for journeys (he used to read the labels on tins and, using the world map on his wall, worked out the route needed to transport the goods to his father's shop). Raised by a strict Roman Catholic father, Hitchcock acquired an acute sensitivity for right and wrong. He also learnt about fear at the age of five, when his father sent Hitchcock to the police station with a note. The policeman read the note, then locked Hitchcock in a cell for five minutes. Upon release, Hitchcock was told that this is what they do to naughty little boys. It is not surprising that this led Hitch to later feature the police as fearful characters. Think of Janet Leigh in *Psycho*, stealing $40,000, and waking up in her car with a cop staring through the window. Morally we should be applauding the good work of Mr Policeman, but emotionally we fear for Janet.

At St Ignatius' College, a Jesuit boarding school, Hitchcock learnt about discipline, self-control and organisation (which led to Hitch's later daily routine, always wearing the same style of suit, the methodical approach to work), and also the sadistic physical punishment used to attain that discipline. Hitch used his fear of pain to make the violent parts of his movies more affecting.

After training as an engineer (hence his appreciation for the technical aspects of movie-making), Hitch moved into graphic design, working at a small advertising company, and then onto W T Henley, a cable company. Having acquired a love for films, through a friend at Henley's, Hitch began working part-time designing captions and titles for silent films. Then he got a full-time post as chief of the title department at Famous Players-Lasky where, during 1921-1922, he titled nearly a dozen films. In 1922, aged 23, Hitchcock became a director and producer, albeit for an ill-fated production. His first directorial stint was an independent production called *Number Thirteen*. The film was a comedy about London low life starring Clare Greet, who put up some of the money for the project. However, it was not enough to sustain the project and the film was never completed. Hitch subsequently cast Clare Greet in many of his films.

Then Hitch got his break. Seymour Hicks was playing the lead in a film of his play when the director and screenwriter Hugh Croise fell ill. Desperate to finish, Hicks co-directed with the enthusiastic Hitch on *Always Tell Your Wife* which was released in 1923. Then, with Graham Cutts as director and Michael Balcon as producer, Hitch was designer, assistant director and scriptwriter on five movies up until 1925. Some of these were made at Germany's UFA studios, the heart of Expressionistic film-making and home to some of the best technicians in the world. Balcon was impressed with Hitch and wanted him to direct, but film distributors were wary of new names, so Balcon had Hitch direct a couple of films in Germany's Emelka studios and on location around Europe. Hitchcock's career had started.

The Pleasure Garden (1925)

Cast: Virginia Valli (Patsy Brand), Carmelita Geraghty (Jill Cheyne), Miles Mander (Levett), John Stuart (Hugh Fielding), Nita Naldi (Native)

Crew: Director Alfred Hitchcock, Screenplay Eliot Stannard, Novel Oliver Sandys, Producers Michael Balcon & Erich Pommer, Cinematographer Baron Ventimiglia, Assistant Director Alma Reville

Story: Good girl Patsy Brand, a chorus girl at The Pleasure Garden Theatre, marries Levett, a soldier of fortune, who is going to the English colonies in the Tropics with his friend Hugh. Before leaving for her honeymoon she meets Jill, Hugh's fiancée, and gets her a job in the theatre. Jill is a bad girl and goes out with other men. When Patsy finds out her husband is ill, she goes to the Tropics, but finds Levett an alcoholic living with a native girl. Levett drowns the native girl, saying it was suicide, then tries to kill Patsy. A doctor enters, shoots Levett and gets the girl. Sound awful? Well, at least it has a duality theme.

And Another Thing: This was made in 1925, but it was not released until 1927 because the film distributor, H M Woolf, thought that since Hitch had filmed it in the style of the German Expressionists with weird angles, English audiences would not be able to understand it.

Comment: Although *The Lodger* is the first true Hitchcock movie because it's about a murder, it's a suspense thriller and so on, *The Pleasure Garden* obviously contained some elements which Hitch would later develop in full. We have the duality of the good/bad girl (*Vertigo* comes to mind), the psychological aspect (virtually every Hitchcock film) and of course a source material which is adapted by Hitch to fit his own worldview.

The Mountain Eagle (1926)

Alternative Title: Fear O' God (1926) in USA

Cast: Nita Naldi (Beatrice), Bernhard Goetzke (Pettigrew), John F Hamilton (Edward Pettigrew), Malcolm Keen (Fear o' God Fulton)

Crew: Director Alfred Hitchcock, Screenplay Eliot Stannard, Producer Michael Balcon, Cinematographer Baron Ventimiglia

Story: Pettigrew, a shopkeeper in a mountain town of Kentucky, falls in love with teacher Beatrice. The girl doesn't reciprocate, so he gets angry and accuses her of molesting his son Edward who has a mental illness The girl marries the hermit, Fear o' God Fulton, to calm the people's anger and, eventually, she falls in love with her husband and a child is born. Pettigrew hides Edward and charges the hermit with his son's murder. Fear o' God is imprisoned but he escapes and takes refuge in the mountain with his wife and son.

The Lodger (1926)

Alternative Title: The Case Of Jonathan Drew (1926)

Cast: Ivor Novello (The Lodger), June Tripp (Daisy Bunting, a Mannequin), Malcolm Keen (Joe Betts, a Police Detective), Marie Ault (The Landlady, Mrs Bunting), Arthur Chesney (Her Husband, Mr Bunting), Helena Pick (Anne Rowley)

Crew: Director Alfred Hitchcock, Screenplay Eliot Stannard & Alfred Hitchcock, Novel Marie Bellot Lowndes, Producers Michael Balcon & Carlyle Blackwell Sr., Cinematographer Baron Ventimiglia, Film Editing Ivor Montagu, Assistant Director Alma Reville, Editing/Titling Ivor Montagu, Title Designer E McKnight Kauffer

Blonde Virgin: June Tripp.

Story: The Avenger kills blondes every Tuesday. A mysterious stranger takes lodgings at the Buntings' house. Their girl Daisy takes a shine to him. The lodger leaves the house late Tuesday, and the next murder occurs. Daisy's boyfriend, a Scotland Yard detective, suspects the lodger and arrests him. The lodger escapes with Daisy, is chased by a crowd and is almost killed by them.

Visual Ideas: A man's face is distorted in a tea urn. When two men deliver newspapers in a van, their heads in the windows are like the pupils of eyes. The lodger is seen walking up and down his room through a glass ceiling. Looking straight down a stairwell, we see a hand holding the rail, circling as a character descends the stairs.

Recurring Motif: The flashing neon sign 'To-Night Golden Curls' is repeated throughout the movie, as a sign of the constant presence of The Avenger. At the end, The Avenger is imprisoned, the hero and heroine kiss in the bright light, whilst the neon sign still flashes in the black night behind them.

Recurring Ideas: The Kiss (Pure, close-up, slow, white); The Handcuffs (A sign that the man is outside society); The Switch (For the first half of the movie, the lodger is dressed in black and placed in shadows, so we don't trust/like him. After the murder, and the family suspect him of being The Avenger, the lodger is dressed in nice, light clothes and his room is bright, so we like/trust him); The Hanging Man (At the end, the villain is hanging, but is saved by the hero).

The Walk-On: Hitch always maintained that his cameo roles were a bit of fun at first, and then it became a superstition. Finally, when the public expected it, he got them over with as soon as possible. This film has two Hitch appearances. First, he is seated at a newsroom - Hitch said they needed someone to fill the space, and Hitch was big enough to fill it. Later, wearing a cap, he's seen leaning against the railings when Ivor Novello is caught.

The Verdict: If you can watch silent movies, you'll love this one. 4/5

Downhill (1927)

Alternative Title: When Boys Leave Home (1928) in USA

Cast: Ivor Novello (Roddy Berwick), Robin Irvine (Tim Wakely), Lilian Braithwaite (Lady Berwick), Isabel Jeans (Julia Hannah Jones), Ian Hunter (Archie), Sybil Rhoda (Sybil Wakely), Ben Webster (Doctor Dowson)

Crew: Director Alfred Hitchcock, Screenplay Eliot Stannard, Play David Lestrange (pseudonym for Constance Collier & Ivor Novello), Producer Michael Balcon, Cinematographer Claude L McDonnell, Film Editing Ivor Montagu

Story: Roddy, first son of the rich Berwick family, is expelled from school when he takes the blame for his friend Tim's theft. His family sends him away and all of his friends stay away from him. Roddy goes to Paris, spends all his money, starts work as a dancer and becomes an alcoholic. Roddy moves to an English colony but some sailors return him to his rich family hoping for a reward.

Easy Virtue (1927)

Cast: Isabel Jeans (Larita Filton), Franklin Dyall (Her husband, M Filton), Ian Hunter (The Plaintiff's Counsel), Robin Irvine (John Whittaker), Violet Farebrother (His mother), Eric Bransby Williams (The Correspondent)

Crew: Director Alfred Hitchcock, Screenplay Eliot Stannard, Play Noel Coward, Producer Michael Balcon, Cinematographer Claude L McDonnell, Film Editing Ivor Montagu

Story: Larita Filton is accused by her husband of being in love with an artist. There is a scandalous divorce case and the artist kills himself. Larita's world is destroyed so she decides to change her identity and start a new life. She falls in love with and marries a rich young man, John Whittaker. John's mother finds out about Larita's 'easy virtue' and tells her son everything.

The Ring (1927)

Cast: Carl Brisson (Jack Sanders aka One Round Jack), Lillian Hall-Davis (Nelly), Ian Hunter (Bob Corby, The Champion)

Crew: Director & Scenario Alfred Hitchcock, Adaptation Alma Reville, Producer John Maxwell, Cinematographer Jack E Cox

Story: One Round Jack is a boxer who fights in bazaars. He is engaged to Nelly. Without revealing his true identity, the Australian champion Bob Corby, who is falling in love with Nelly, challenges Jack. Jack loses and Bob, who wants to be close to Nelly, hires Jack as his sparring partner. A short time passes until Bob and Nelly run away together. Jack is now in training for his revenge. He challenges Bob in the Albert Hall.

The Farmer's Wife (1928)

Cast: Jameson Thomas (Farmer Samuel Sweetland), Lillian Hall-Davis (Araminta Dench, the Housekeeper)

Crew: Director Alfred Hitchcock, Screenplay Leslie Arliss & Alfred Hitchcock & J E Hunter & Norman Lee & Eliot Stannard, Play Eden Philpotts, Producer John Maxwell, Cinematographer Jack E Cox, Film Editing Alfred Booth

Story: Farmer Sweetland is an old and lonely widower who, after his daughter marries, feels he should marry again. With the aid of Minta, his house maid (who is secretly in love with him), Sweetland comes up with a list of four ladies and, one by one, they reject him. Returning home, he thinks of each of them by his side and sees them as ridiculous. Then, for the first time, he sees Minta and proposes.

Visual Ideas: The passage of time is shown by the number of times the farmer's underclothes have been washed, or the time it takes the meat to cook in front of the fire. There is also a well-edited collage of scenes for when the farmer is getting washed and dressed for courting.

The Verdict: Excellent photography and earthy dialogue are the only things to keep you awake watching this, since the version I saw has no sound or music. 2/5

Champagne (1928)

Cast: Betty Balfour (Betty), Jean Bradin (The Boy), Theo von Alten (The Man), Gordon Harker (The Father)

Crew: Director Alfred Hitchcock, Screenplay Eliot Stannard, Story Walter C Mycroft, Adaptation Alfred Hitchcock, Producer John Maxwell, Cinematographer Jack E Cox, Still Photographer Michael Powell

Story: Betty, rebellious spoilt daughter of a millionaire, decides to marry the penniless Jean against her father's will. She runs away to France and lives a life of luxury on the profits from her father's champagne business. Her father decides to put a stop to her behaviour by pretending his business crashed. Betty now has to earn money and she gets a job in a nightclub.

The Manxman (1929)

Cast: Anny Ondra (Kate Cregeen), Carl Brisson (Pete Quilliam), Malcolm Keen (Philip Christian), Randle Ayrton (Caesar Cregeen), Clare Greet (Mother)

Crew: Director Alfred Hitchcock, Screenplay Eliot Stannard, Novel Hall Caine, Producer John Maxwell, Cinematographer Jack E Cox, Film Editing Emile de Ruelle, Still Photographer Michael Powell

Story: Despite their differing backgrounds, fisherman Pete and lawyer Philip have been lifelong friends on the Isle of Man. Pete wants to marry Kate, the landlord's daughter at the local inn. However Kate's father doesn't think he is good enough. Pete leaves the island to seek his fortune abroad and entrusts Kate to Philip, who become attracted to each other.

2. The Mastermind Returns (1929-1939)

Hitch had been wandering around aimlessly for a couple of years making films with all kinds of subject matter, with varying levels of success. In truth, the promise he showed in *The Lodger* had failed to materialise. Then he directed *Blackmail*, one of Britain's first talkies. Originally filmed silent (a silent version was made for those cinemas who could not afford the expensive sound equipment), at the last minute the producer decided to add sound on the last reel. Instead, Hitch spread the sound throughout the film, and this impressed the production company so much he was allowed to reshoot several key scenes with sound. However, there was a major problem - Anny Ondra had a thick German accent. So Hitch had Anny mouth the words, and another actress, Joan Barry, say the words into a microphone. These solutions showed two important qualities in Hitch which enabled him to rise higher and higher within the film community - he knew how to impress producers, and he knew how to solve technical difficulties when making films. The third quality - how to impress the audience - he learnt when he began making his Wrong Man/Man On The Run movies in the early 1930s with the writer Charles Bennett.

Blackmail (1929)

Cast: Anny Ondra (Alice White), Joan Barry (Voice of Alice White), Sara Allgood (Mrs White), Charles Paton (Mr White), John Longden (Detective Frank Webber), Donald Calthrop (Tracy, the Blackmailer), Cyril Ritchard (The Artist)

Crew: Director & Screenplay Alfred Hitchcock, Dialogue Benn W Levy & Michael Powell, Play Charles Bennett, Producer John Maxwell, Original Music Hubert Bath & Campbell Connelly, Cinematographer Jack E Cox, Film Editing Emile de Ruelle

Blonde Virgin: Anny Ondra.

The MacGuffin: Coined by Angus MacPhail for *The 39 Steps*, this is the mysterious objective around which the plot revolves. In this case, a glove left by Alice at the scene of the murder is what everybody's looking for.

Story: Alice two-times her Scotland Yard detective boyfriend by going with an artist. The artist tries it on in his garret, and Alice knifes him. Shocked, distraught, she makes it home. Her detective boyfriend finds her glove at the murder scene but covers up for her, only to find out Tracy, who has the other glove, wants to blackmail them. Our fearless detective bluffs Tracy into making a run for it. A chase ensues through the British Museum. Alice, racked with guilt, tries to confess but events contrive to let her go free with her boyfriend.

Visual Ideas: As the cops enter a room, a man is on the bed, reading the paper, oblivious to the cops. Then the camera pans from his face to a mirror, then zooms into the mirror, where we can see the faces of the cops. Time passing is shown by the number of cigarette butts in the ashtray. As Alice and the artist mount the stairs, from side on, the camera travels up. As the artist is about to attack Alice, he pauses and the light and shadow of the lamp falls on his face, distorting half his face, as though revealing an inner demon. When Alice is in the artist's garret, she sees a policeman walk by in the street, so she thinks she's safe but, as she's being attacked, the policeman walks by and can do nothing to help her. When a description of the blackmailer is circulated by the police, a montage of mugshots and the various books slide in and out of the frame, until the blackmailer's face looms large. When Alice decides to give herself up, she writes a confession letter and rises - as she rises, the shadow of a noose fails around her neck. When she enters the artist's room, Alice laughs at the funny clown painting laughing and pointing at her, but after the murder, the clown is laughing at her and later, when her confession is not heard, the picture is there again, laughing at her.

Audio Ideas: Every possible sound is used - music, whistling, horns, birds, cars. At one stage, our detective hero whistles 'Sonny Boy,' a cheeky reference to *The Jazz Singer* of the previous year - the first talkie. Some of the dialogue is well written and surprisingly natural. The high-pitched twittering of the bird in Alice's room annoys her. The doorbell of Alice's tobacconist shop is loud and distorted, creating an unsettling effect when people enter. At breakfast Alice is asked to cut the bread - the knife and bread are like the knife and bread beside the dead artist's bed. As Alice picks up the knife, a neighbour babbles on about the murder using the word "knife" all the time, her words getting softer and lower, but the word knife staying loud, so all Alice hears is "KNIFE." Surprisingly, the slimy blackmailer has a posh voice, a sign of educated villains to come.

Recurring Ideas: The Procedure (The apprehension and processing of the criminal is shown from police van to lock-up); The Double Scene (Hitchcock shows a scene at the beginning, the hunting of the criminal, and then repeats it later on, our expectations of the outcome conflicting with our desire - we want the villain to be caught and he probably will be, but he'll blow the gaffe on Alice, whom we like); The Outstretched Hand

(When the artist tries to kill Alice, her hand stretches out from behind the curtain, desperately flailing, before falling upon a knife with which she kills him. The outstretched arm of the dead man also reoccurs throughout); Handcuffs; The Switch (At the beginning we don't like Alice because she's two-timing the detective but, after she kills the artist, perversely, we sympathise with her and don't want her caught); The Public Finale (The blackmailer is chased through the British Museum, clambers down a ladder by a giant face, ends up on the roof and falls through the skylight); Never The Same Again (At the end, Alice and Frank leave the police station. They do not hold hands, or embrace. A distance has entered their relationship).

The Walk-On: Trying to read a book on the underground train, Hitch is bothered by a little boy à la W C Fields.

And Another Thing: Michael Powell, later of famous film partnership Powell & Pressburger, was the stills photographer on *Blackmail* and other Hitchcock films.

The Verdict: It would have been aesthetically better is Mr Hitchcock had left this one silent - the pacing is atrocious, mainly because of lengthy static dialogue sequences. However, there are occasional glimpses of brilliance in his use of sound. 3/5

Elstree Calling (1930)

Cast: Donald Calthrop, Gordon Harker, Nathan Shacknovsky, John Stuart, Jameson Thomas, Anna May Wong (Herself)

Crew: Directors André Charlot & Alfred Hitchcock (some sketches) & Jack Hulbert & Paul Murray, Screenplay Val Valentine, Original Music Reg Casson & Vivian Ellis & Chic Endor, Lyrics Ivor Novello & Jack Strachey Parsons, Cinematographer Claude Friese-Greene, Supervising Director Adrian Brunel

Story: This was Britain's first musical - basically a cobbled-together sprinkling of variety acts and musical numbers. Hitch's contribution was the framing device of a family (the father played by Gordon Harker) trying to watch the show on their television set (at that time TV would have been more science fiction than fact). Apparently, Hitch did not spend more than 7 hours on the set.

The Verdict: Don't bother. 0/5

Juno And The Paycock (1930)

Alternative Title: The Shame Of Mary Boyle

Cast: Sara Allgood (Juno), Edward Chapman (Captain Boyle), Maire O'Neill (Mrs Madigan), Sidney Morgan (Joxer), John Longden (Chris Bentham), John Laurie (Johnny Boyle), Donald Calthrop (Needle Nugent), Barry Fitzgerald (The Orator)

Crew: Director Alfred Hitchcock, Screenplay Alfred Hitchcock & Alma Reville, Play Sean O'Casey, Producer John Maxwell, Cinematographer Jack E Cox, Film Editing Emile de Ruelle

Story: During the Irish revolution, a family earns a big inheritance. They start leading a rich life forgetting what the most important values are.

And Another Thing: Using the original cast of the successful Abbey Theatre production, Hitch got O'Casey to write a new scene in a pub at the beginning, but it's basically a film of the stage play. Hitch was embarrassed about the vast amount of praise he received for something that didn't really have his stamp on it. Hitch directed *Mary* (1930), a German version, with a different cast.

Murder! (1930)

Cast: Herbert Marshall (Sir John Menier), Norah Baring (Diana Baring), Phyllis Konstam (Doucie Markham, Doucebelle Dear), Edward Chapman (Ted Markham), Miles Mander (Gordon Druce), Esme Percy (Handel Fane), Donald Calthrop (Ion Stewart), Clare Greet (Jury Member)

Crew: Director Alfred Hitchcock, Adaptation Alfred Hitchcock & Walter C Mycroft, Screenplay Alma Reville, Novel *Enter Sir John* Clemence Dane & Helen Simpson, Producer John Maxwell, Original Music John Reynders, Cinematographer Jack E Cox, Film Editing Rene Marrison & Emile de Ruelle

Story: An actress is found guilty of murder and is sentenced to hang. One of the jury, Sir John Menier, an acting impresario à la Noel Coward, regrets his decision and decides to investigate the actors, scene of crime etc. with the help of the acting troupe. Sir John tries to trap the villain by auditioning him for a murder mystery, based on the real murder, where the villain plays the murderer and must fill in the missing clues. The villain doesn't fall for it. Later, when cornered, the villain commits suicide.

Visual Ideas: Opens with two tracking shots. The first is looking into the upper windows of a street as people look out the window in response to screams. The second is a murder tableau - an immobile crowd is looking at the murdered woman on the floor. The camera, slowly, painfully moves from one face/body to the other, eventually following the arm/hand of the murderess to the poker and the dead body. A seminal shot - used by Martin Scorsese, David Lynch, Brian De Palma etc. When a stage manager walks across Sir John Menier's office, the floor is made of sponge. When looking for the villain Fane, a vane is shown because they are looking in all directions, as the accused woman is circling her cell, as the shadow of the hanging rope rises up a wall.

Audio Ideas: During the jury's deliberation, they pressure Sir John Menier to vote 'guilty' in rhyme/rhythm. Sir John's thoughts are spoken to us in a stream of consciousness manner. Music is used as background rhythm to his thoughts.

Subtext: Great emphasis is made of people putting on and taking off clothes. The opening shot is people putting on clothes. The actors exchange costumes whilst performing. The Markhams put on their Sunday best to meet Sir John. This changing of identity/rôle is further confused by women in male rôles: the female barrister and the jury women as experts on psychology. Identity, specifically sexual identity, is the theme of the movie. The villain turns out to be an effeminate man who lets his fiancée take the rap for his murder - he's an actor who falls back on his old drag trapeze-artist act to make money. He killed because he is a half caste, which is weak. Saying he was gay would have made more sense of his actions/rôle throughout the picture, and have been more interesting psychologically.

Recurring Ideas: The Hanging Man; The Public Finale (At the end, the villain, a drag trapeze artist, hangs himself in front of the circus crowd).

The Walk-On: Passer-by on the street.

The Verdict: Despite interesting experiments, boring, overacted, static, stilted. In two words: a dog. 2/5

The Skin Game (1931)

Cast: C V France (Mr Hillcrest), Helen Haye (Mrs Hillcrest), Jill Esmond (Jill Hillcrest), Edmund Gwenn (Mr Hornblower), John Longden (Charles Hornblower), Phyllis Konstam (Chloe Hornblower), Frank Lawton (Rolf Hornblower)

Crew: Director & Adaptation Alfred Hitchcock, Screenplay Alma Reville, Play John Galsworthy, Producer John Maxwell, Cinematographer Jack E Cox, Film Editing A Gobett, Clapper Boy Jack Cardiff

Story: Two families, one country gentry the other nouveaux riches industrialists, fight over a piece of land. Blackmail is involved.

The Verdict: Static, stagnant, boring. 0/5

Rich And Strange (1932)

Alternative Title: East Of Shanghai (1932) in USA

Cast: Henry Kendall (Fred Hill), Joan Barry (Emily Hill), Percy Marmont (Commander Gordon), Betty Amann (The Princess), Elsie Randolph (The Old Maid), Aubrey Dexter (Colonel)

Crew: Director & Adaptation Alfred Hitchcock, Screenplay Alma Reville, Additional Dialogue Val Valentine, Idea Dale Collins, Producer John Maxwell, Original Music Hal Dolphe, Musical Director John Reynders, Cinematographer Jack E Cox & Charles Martin, Film Editing Winifred Cooper & Rene Marrison

Blonde Virgin: Joan Barry.

The MacGuffin: Err, this is a romantic comedy - they don't have MacGuffins.

Story: Accountant's Clerk Fred Hill (could it represent Alfred H?) and his wife Emily (Alma?) want out of their dreary middle-class life and yearn for a life of adventure on the high seas. They get it courtesy of a rich uncle. Fred and Em cross the channel, do Paris and then travel by boat from Marseilles to Port Said, Colombo and Singapore. Fred, being prone to seasickness, spends a lot of his time in bed, while Em is romanced by Commander Gordon. When Fred recovers after a miracle cure from a comedic old maid, he promptly falls for the charms of The Princess. They pair off and as Em is leaving with Gordon, she discovers The Princess is a con-artist and returns to Fred, only to find The Princess has done a bunk with all their money. Now poor, the Hills take a cheap steamer home, which promptly sinks. Fearing it is all over, they declare their love for each other. They survive, are picked up by a Chinese junk, witness the death of a Chinese man and the birth of a baby. Returning to their dreary home, they begin bickering about arrangements for the baby they plan to have.

Visual Ideas: The opening scene in the Accounts office begins with a close-up of a ledger, and pans up to the office with all the people crammed behind desks, then pans around as they leave and everyone goes down the stairs. When Fred first encounters seasickness, he is trying to take a photo of Em and, through the viewfinder, we see Em's picture juggling around. He sees a film of spots when he looks at Em, and these spots turn to plates. Later, when Em reads a goodbye letter from Gordon and is crying, we see the letter but it is blurred as if by tears - Gordon's voice-over reads the letter for us. Earlier, when Em and Gordon are getting to know each other, Hitch signals their growing closeness with a sweet bit of business - Em takes a photo of Gordon sitting down and playfully draws a female figure in the empty chair beside him, which triggers the idea in our minds, and in Em's, that a romance is beginning. When the ship is sinking, Hitch remains focused on the couple in their cabin, the water rising in the porthole and seeping under the door, gunshots and shouting penetrating the walls, giving a fearfully claustrophobic feeling to the movie. Hitch later repeated this idea in *Foreign Correspondent*. As Fred and Em escape onto the junk, one of the Chinese men gets caught in a rope and drowns, his colleagues looking on dispassionately - we see them from the side (another Hitchcock image to be repeated time and time again).

Audio Ideas: Ironically, when Fred decides to leave Em, people are singing 'For He's A Jolly Good fellow' in the background. And when he decides to go back to Em, a band is playing joyful music outside the hotel.

Recurring Ideas: The Journey (Hitch's later couples would make journeys across the world, often on the run, where they have to learn to love each other. In fact, the journey in this movie was inspired by Hitch's 1931 round-the-world trip with his wife and daughter. And the Paris sequences were based on Hitch's honeymoon misadventures with Alma).

Subtext. This is a rites of passage movie, where the intelligent and sensitive Em learns that she loves Fred, and Fred learns what a fool and buffoon he really is. In the end, no matter how rich they are, or how strange their experiences, they seem to have learnt nothing, and revert to type when they return home.

The Verdict: After a promising start, it's too uneven and bizarre in places to totally engage us, but it does hint at the dark comedy that was to come. 2/5

Number Seventeen (1932)

Cast: Leon M Lion (Ben), Anne Grey (The Girl), John Stuart (The Detective), Donald Calthrop (Brant), Barry Jones (Henry Doyle), Ann Casson (Rose Ackroyd), Henry Caine (Mr Ackroyd), Garry Marsh (Sheldrake)

Crew: Director Alfred Hitchcock, Screenplay Rodney Ackland & Alfred Hitchcock & Alma Reville, Novel Joseph Jefferson Farjeon, Producer John Maxwell, Original Music A Hallis, Cinematographers Jack E Cox & Bryan Langley, Film Editing A C Hammond

The MacGuffin: A jewelled necklace.

Story: It's difficult to describe this one because almost all the characters don't have names. Anyway, the man who later is revealed as The Detective goes into a darkened house where he discovers a salty seaman, a dead body, the dead body's daughter, three villains looking over the house and a villain in the back room. There are a couple of fights, gunplay, and the girl and detective get tied up. Eventually, they all end up on a train or chasing the train in a bus. It's totally ludicrous, but eminently watchable.

Visual Ideas: Starts with long tracking shot of a hat rolling in the wind and leaves (later borrowed by The Coen Brothers for *Miller's Crossing*), stopping at a garden gate. A man, his back to us, picks up the hat, looks up, sees a light flickering in the dark house, walks up to the door, tries it, it opens, walks in, walks up to the stairs and quickly looks up. Shadows appear and move along the walls: a giant hand, a web, a shadow hand grabbing a doorknob. Several times, the swish of the wind is accompanied by a shot of a window, an extremely fast pan, as if the camera were following the wind, to a candle being extinguished by the gust. We look down the centre of the stairs as a hand on the rail slides around and around, coming up towards us. The fight is hand to hand, very close in, silent - looking from above a hand is on a chin, pushing the head back. The bodies switch around during the fight, so that the wrong man is hit.

Audio Ideas: When a dead body is discovered, the wide open mouth and distorted face of a scream are covered by the screaming whistle of a train going by. The dialogue is very good, very sharp, very natural - the first well-written Hitchcock film.

Recurring Ideas: The Hanging Man (When tied to the banister, it breaks, and the detective and the girl are left dangling between the stairs); The Mute Woman (The brunette Nora is introduced as being deaf and dumb, for no apparent reason, but then turns out not to be so); The Great Train Race (The train carrying the villains must get to the night ferry to the continent. On the train, there is a fight for the jewels, a pursuit, hanging from the side of the train, as the train races neck and neck with the hero in the hijacked bus); Handcuffs (Called bracelets in this one, the brunette Nora is cuffed and drowning at the end, but is saved by our hero).

And Another Thing: Hitchcock did not want to direct this one, and conceived it as a burlesque - the mute woman (the heroine is always dumb, why not literally?), the villains calling to see the house after midnight, the train chase using models (meant to be derisory but actually quite effective).

The Verdict: A fast-moving, running-about-a-deserted-house, adding-a-character-every-five-minutes type of movie that works because it twists and turns before we have time to think. 3/5

Waltzes From Vienna (1933)

Alternative Title: Strauss' Great Waltz (1935) in USA

Cast: Hindle Edgar (Leopold), Sybil Grove (Mme Fouchett), Edmund Gwenn (Strauss the Elder), Robert Hale (Ebezeder), Esmond Knight (Strauss the Younger), Jessie Matthews (Rasi), Frank Vosper (The Prince)

Crew: Director Alfred Hitchcock, Screenplay Guy Bolton & Alma Reville, Play Guy Bolton, Music Johann Strauss Sr. & Johann Strauss, Cinematographer Glen MacWilliams

The Verdict: Hitchcock was unemployable for a time and, at his lowest ebb, took on a subject for which he had no affinity - a musical about Strauss senior and Strauss junior. All the stars, like Jessie Matthews and Esmond Knight later commented how perfectly dreadful Hitch was during filming although, by all reports, the film is quite nice with a few Hitchcock moments.

The Man Who Knew Too Much (1934)

Cast: Leslie Banks (Bob Lawrence), Edna Best (Jill Lawrence), Peter Lorre (Abbott), Frank Vosper (Ramon), Hugh Wakefield (Clive), Nova Pilbeam (Betty Lawrence), Pierre Fresnay (Louis Bernard), Joan Harrison (Secretary)

Crew: Director Alfred Hitchcock, Scenario Edwin Greenwood & A R Rawlinson, Additional Dialogue Charles Bennett & D B Wyndham-Lewis & Emlyn Williams, Producers Michael Balcon & Ivor Montagu, Original Music Arthur Benjamin, Musical Director Louis Levy, Cinematographer Curt Courant, Film Editing Hugh Stewart

Blonde Virgin: Edna Best.

The MacGuffin: The Assassination.

Story: Jill and Bob Lawrence are vacationing in St Moritz with their daughter when they witness the assassination of a secret agent, who tells them of a plot to kill a foreign diplomat in London. Their daughter is kidnapped by the spy ring, led by Abbott, to ensure their silence. The couple go to London to track down the kidnappers, and Jill cries out during the concert at the Albert Hall, thus preventing the assassination. Jill, who is an expert shot (as established at the beginning of the film), then goes in guns blazing to rescue her daughter. The climax is a gun battle between the spies and the police, reminiscent of the celebrated 1911 Siege of Sidney Street.

Recurring Ideas: The Cultured Villain.

And Another Thing: This was Peter Lorre's first role in English. Hitch had seen Lorre play the whistling child murderer in Fritz Lang's *M*, since which Lorre had decided to leave Germany due to the attentions of a certain Mr Hitler.

The Verdict: Tougher, faster and more interesting than the later remake, this was Hitchcock's initial template for future thriller films. 3/5

The 39 Steps (1935)

Cast: Robert Donat (Richard Hannay), Madeleine Carroll (Pamela), Lucie Mannheim (Annabella Smith), Godfrey Tearle (Professor Jordan), Peggy Ashcroft (Margaret), John Laurie (John), Helen Haye (Mrs Jordan), Wylie Watson (Mr Memory), Gus McNaughton (Commercial Traveller)

Crew: Director Alfred Hitchcock, Adaptation Charles Bennett, Continuity Alma Reville, Dialogue Ian Hay, Novel John Buchan, Producers Michael Balcon & Ivor Montagu, Original Music Hubert Bath, Musical Director Louis Levy, Cinematographer Bernard Knowles, Film Editing Derek N Twist

Blonde Virgin: Madeleine Carroll.

The MacGuffin: A silent aeroplane engine.

Story: Hannay picks up a woman during a fight at a London music hall, but she ends up dead and Hannay is framed for her murder. Whilst being hunted, he follows the clues to a place in Scotland near Killin (nice pun) and finds the suave villain of the piece, who promptly shoots Hannay. Saved by a very thick *Bible*, Hannay goes to the police and ends up on the run again, back to London. This time, he's picked up by the villains and accompanied by a disbelieving Pamela - they end up handcuffed together and on the run from the villains. Ensconced in a pub, Pamela discovers Hannay is telling the truth and they track down the villain to the Palladium. Mr Memory turns up on the bill. Hannay asks what are the 39 steps. "…a secret organisation of spies for…" Mr Memory is shot by the villain, the villain is caught, Mr Memory dies and Hannay and Pamela hold hands.

Visual Ideas: Where to start? The film starts by following the feet of a man into a music hall (neon sign) whom we later find out is our hero. As Hannay escapes on the train, his pursuers' legs run after the shadow of the train. As Hannay and Carroll are being escorted in a car by the villains, dialogue flowing, there's a great pan from the front of the car around to the back that cuts seamlessly into a shot of the back of the car driving off down the winding Scottish Highland roads.

Audio Ideas: When the body of the woman is discovered, the cleaner (who looks like the screaming woman from Eisenstein's Odessa Steps sequence in *Battleship Potemkin*) turns to scream, but her wide open mouth turns into a railway tunnel and the train coming out of the tunnel is whistling/screaming for her. At the crofter's hut, the suspicious crofter goes outside, looks back through a window and sees his wife and Hannay talking animatedly, and thinks them lovers because he cannot hear their words - the irony, of course, is that silence is being used in the talkies. As Hannay escapes from the Sheriff, he jumps through a window and into a crowd - Hannay is afraid and trapped in the jeering crowd, the jeering could almost be for Hannay. When Mr Memory is dying his words are accompanied by cheerful music as the chorus girls dance in the background.

Subtext: This film is about betrayal and the lack of trust, and the reasons why people do what they do. At every stage of the chase, Hannay is betrayed or trusted by everyone, depending upon their prejudices and assumptions, not on his word or appearance. A milkman doesn't believe that a woman has been killed in Hannay's apartment and spies are after him, but helps Hannay because he understands the idea of Hannay having an illicit affair and wanting to dodge the husband and brother. On the train, Hannay, on the run from police, kisses Pamela to hide his face - she takes umbrage and promptly tells the police "this is the man you want." The crofter only takes Hannay in for money and, when the police come, turns him in for the reward. The man Hannay tracks down to prove his innocence turns out to be the villain, who promptly shoots Hannay. The Sheriff turns Hannay in because he trusts the villain, a respected local man. The publican wife and husband protect Hannay and Pamela from the villains because again, they believe them to be a love couple eloping since they always hold hands (because of the handcuffs). There are people who say they are police, when they are not - people trust the police. Hannay is assumed to be a politician, when he is not. Mr Memory remembers all the details of the silent engine both for money, and also for the professional challenge - his professionalism is his undoing because he cannot refuse to answer a question.

Recurring Ideas: The Public Place (The Music Hall, the Palladium); The Smart-Aleck Crowd (At the Music Hall, political rally and the Palladium there are lots of one-liners and a sense of community); The Psychological Explanation (Hannay says that the woman he picked up at the beginning of the film suffers from "persecution mania"); The Defect (Hannay knows that the man with the top of his little finger missing is the villain); The Shock Twist (The woman Hannay meets and we have grown to like, is killed, a knife in the back, in Hannay's apartment. This is a real shock, we thought she was going to be the romantic interest. A precursor to *Psycho*?); The Wrong Man/The Man On The Run; Trains; Technology (Hitchcock, bizarrely, has a shot of an autogiro scouring the Highlands in search of Hannay); The Cultured Villain (Professor Jordan is a respected figure, has a cultured voice, a simple, matter-of-fact way of explaining things and is always calm, fatherly); The Family Of Villains (The villain's wife, servants and probably children know the villain is a villain, and support him. They carry on with a normal family life - a chilling view of life if you think about it); Handcuffs (Ends with Hannay and Pamela holding hands); The Recurring Tune (Hannay hears the entrance music for Mr Memory, whistles it occasionally throughout the film and, at The Palladium, recognises it from the music hall at the beginning of the film. Although never stated, it gives the reason why all the spies were in the music hall in the first place).

The Walk-On: Passer-by on the street.

The Verdict: A sparkling script, engaging characters and razor-sharp editing make this just as enjoyable today as when it was first shown over 60 years ago. Hitchcock's first masterpiece. 5/5

Secret Agent (1936)

Cast: John Gielgud (Edgar Brodie/Richard Ashenden), Peter Lorre (The General), Madeleine Carroll (Elsa Carrington), Robert Young (Robert Marvin), Percy Marmont (Caypor), Florence Kahn (Mrs Caypor), Charles Carson ('R'), Lilli Palmer (Lilli), Michael Redgrave (Army Captain)

Crew: Director Alfred Hitchcock, Scenario Charles Bennett, Dialogue Ian Hay, Additional Dialogue Jesse Lasky Jr. & Alma Reville, Play Campbell Dixon, Novel *Ashenden* W Somerset Maugham, Producers

Michael Balcon & Ivor Montagu, Cinematographer Bernard Knowles, Film Editing Charles Frend

Blonde Virgin: Madeleine Carroll, although she loses her virginity to Gielgud.

The MacGuffin: Who knows?

Story: Novelist and soldier Brodie is dead, his coffin attended by a one-armed veteran. But lo, Brodie is alive, reinvented as Ashenden, and embarks on a mission to assassinate a German spy in Switzerland. He is accompanied by gorgeous Elsa Carrington and The General, an assassin with an earring and a frazzled perm. First they kill the wrong bloke - an innocent tourist! - then the villain gets killed by accident in a train crash. What pathetic people they are.

Visual Ideas: There's a lovely transition of a car roaring off and the exhaust fumes dissolving into a sauna scene. The German spies use Swiss chocolate to pass on their messages, so they buy the bars, unwrap them and throw the chocolate into the dustbins. Later, there is even a chase in a chocolate factory.

Audio Ideas: As the innocent man is about to die, his dog, miles away, senses something is about to happen and whines uncontrollably, scratching on the door to get out, eventually howling when his master dies. David Lean used a similar idea 12 years later in his adaptation of *Oliver Twist* when Sykes is killing Nancy and the dog tries to escape. After the death, Hitchcock uses a wall of irritating noise (the local folk performing by rolling coins in dishes) to create a feeling of unease. Another time, in the church, there is a steady, loud note on the organ (the organist lies dead on the keys), which is disconcerting because of its insistence.

Recurring Ideas: The Cultured Villain (Robert Young plays an American who woos Elsa throughout the movie and even gives her a picture of himself with an inked-in dastardly moustache, signed 'to the heroine, from the villain'); Church Bell Tower (Gielgud and Lorre trapped in the church tower, the bell ringing, a dead body below them, leads to Lorre's immortal line, "I'm still blind in this ear"); The Train (Switching compartments, trapped, attacked and crashes).

And Another Thing: Lorre's appearance with moustache, earring, flower in his lapel, is very reminiscent of his rôle, five years later, in *The Maltese Falcon*.

The Verdict: A huge misfire. Unbalanced characters and plot fail to create the right atmosphere. How can you sympathise with people who clown about whilst preparing to commit cold-blooded murder? No, no Mr Hitchcock. 1/5

Sabotage (1936)

Alternative Titles: The Hidden Power (1936), also *A Woman Alone* (1937) in USA

Cast: Sylvia Sidney (Sylvia Verloc), Oskar Homolka (Carl Verloc), Desmond Tester (Mrs Verloc's Young Brother, Stevie), John Loder (Police Sergeant Ted Spencer), Clare Greet, Sara Allgood, Charles Hawtrey, Aubrey Mather

Crew: Director Alfred Hitchcock, Scenario Charles Bennett, Play Campbell Dixon, Novel *The Secret Agent* Joseph Conrad, Dialogue Ian Hay & Jesse Lasky Jr. & Helen Simpson, Additional Dialogue E V H Emmett, Continuity Alma Reville, Producers Michael Balcon & Ivor Montagu, Original Music Louis Levy, Cinematographer Bernard Knowles, Film Editing Charles Frend

Blonde Virgin: Sylvia Sidney.

The MacGuffin: Man With A Bomb.

Story: The lights go out all over London, caused by Mr Verloc's sabotage. He returns to his home/cinema, the Bijou, unnoticed by all except Ted the grocer. Pretending to be asleep, Verloc is awakened by his wife Sylvia, a blonde American grateful to Verloc for his kindness to her little brother Stevie, who lives with them. Ted is a police detective spying on Verloc to see if he is one of the saboteurs who are trying to distract Britain from what's going on abroad.

Later, Verloc is refused his money because people laughed during the power cut instead of being fearful, so Verloc must plant a bomb at Piccadilly Circus during the Lord Mayor's Show. Verloc goes to a bird shop and meets the Professor, who will make the bomb. The bomb is delivered, in the bottom of a birdcage, in a wrapped package, ready to explode at 1.45pm. Verloc is about to deliver the package but Ted wants to ask him questions - so Verloc gets Stevie to deliver the bomb. Stevie is delayed, and dies in the explosion. When Sylvia finds out about Stevie, she faints. When she wakes, in her distress she sees Stevie wherever she goes. She confronts Verloc, knowing him to be the villain, a killer. He pleads with her not to give him away. Distraught, she goes into the cinema, starts laughing at the cartoon with the children and then, when Cock Robin is killed, she returns to the dining room and kills Verloc. Ted discovers her and the body, tells her they'll run away together, but she wants to confess. Meanwhile, the Professor goes to the cinema to dispose of the birdcage - the only evidence linking him to Stevie's death - but is followed by the police. Not wanting to be captured, the Professor blows himself up, and

Verloc's body with him. With no evidence against her, Sylvia and Ted walk off together, free to love each other.

Visual Ideas: The irony of the opening sequence is that Verloc is paid to extinguish light, yet he makes money by using light (the cinema). Verloc is dressed in black throughout, yet hero Ted is dressed in the white grocer's coat or a light raincoat. When Verloc agrees to the bombing he looks at one of the aquarium windows, it turns into a picture of Piccadilly Circus, and then it melts, as if the bomb had exploded. As Verloc leaves the zoo, he is trapped by the cage-like gate, as he is trapped by his need for money and is compelled to set the bomb. The most stunning sequence in this film is from when Sylvia finds out Stevie is dead up to her killing Verloc with the knife. She listens to Verloc plead his case, but he is filmed small, wringing his hands, a coward. She holds the knife and throws it away, echoing the knife scene in *Blackmail*. During the whole sequence, Sylvia is silent and we only see the pain in her face, reacting to the events, as Verloc's words pour from his mouth. The actual knifing is quite ambiguous in some ways - we are unsure if it is an accident, or if Sylvia intended it, or if Verloc thrust himself on it.

Audio Ideas: When the bomb goes off, Hitch immediately cuts to Verloc laughing and saying to Ted "Now everything seems to be all right," making the bombing even more chilling.

Recurring Ideas: Birds (As well as the Professor owning a bird shop and delivering the bomb in a birdcage, Verloc says that Stevie is to deliver both the film & 'package' to "kill two birds with one stone." After hearing of Stevie's death, Mrs Verloc laughs and then cries when watching the animated bird killed on the screen as the song 'Who Killed Cock Robin?' is sung); The Theatre (It's set in a cinema, so we see the performances all the time. Also, the glass windows in the aquarium look like screens); The Switch (Although Verloc puts sand in the generator, he actually comes across sympathetically in the beginning, as a weak man doing bad - he doesn't want any loss of life. Also, Ted is wooing his wife, which is not on. He is also quite homely, gentle, soft, quiet and kind to Stevie. It is only when he is under pressure that he does bad things, not wilfully, but by reacting to events. He doesn't want the bomb, but he doesn't want to get caught. However, when Stevie dies, we hate Verloc, and despise his whining); Married To A Bad Man (Sylvia constantly defends Verloc because of his kindness to Stevie, only to find he caused Stevie's death).

The Verdict: A brooding, superbly photographed film which doesn't quite work because we never focus for long enough on either Verloc or Sylvia or Ted. 3/5

Young And Innocent (1937)

Alternative Title: The Girl Was Young (1938) in USA

Cast: Nova Pilbeam (Erica Burgoyne), Derrick De Marney (Robert Tisdall), Percy Marmont (Col. Burgoyne), Edward Rigby (Old Will), Mary Clare (Erica's Aunt), John Longden (Detective Inspector Kent), George Curzon (Guy), Basil Radford (Erica's Uncle)

Crew: Director Alfred Hitchcock, Scenario Charles Bennett & Edwin Greenwood & Anthony Armstrong, Dialogue Gerald Savory, Continuity Alma Reville, Novel *A Shilling For Candles* Josephine Tey, Producer Edward Black, Original Music Al Goodhart & Al Hoffman & Samuel Lerner, Cinematographer Bernard Knowles, Film Editing Charles Frend

Blonde Virgin: Nova Pilbeam.

The MacGuffin: A coat, and later twitching eyes.

Story: Actress Christine Clay is murdered by a man with twitching eyes. Her body is discovered on a beach by Robert Tisdall who runs off for help but is arrested because a) the belt of his stolen raincoat was the murder weapon, b) as a struggling screenwriter he knew and received money from Miss Clay, and c) she left him £12,000 in her will. Upon hearing that last bit of news, he faints, and is brought around by Erica, the Police Commissioner's daughter. Robert escapes by disguising himself with his solicitor's glasses, and meets up with Erica whilst on the run. At first she is reluctant to help him, but at Tom's Hat, a pull-up for lorry drivers, she finds out that Robert's coat was really stolen and given to a tramp called Old Will. She then believes Robert. After finding the tramp, a car chase ensues, their car enters a mine and falls into the mine shaft. Robert and Will jump from the car and Robert saves Erica from death. The only thing in the coat not belonging to Robert is a matchbook from The Grand Hotel. They all go there (Will the tramp dresses as a gentleman to get in because he's the only one who can recognise the man who gave him the coat), and cannot find the man with the twitching eyes. It is the drummer in the band. Seeing the tramp and the police, the drummer becomes so nervous, he takes too many pills, drums badly, collapses and draws attention to himself, just at the moment when Robert, Erica and Will are leaving escorted by the police. Erica, again being helpful, brings the drummer back to consciousness and when he starts twitching, they all realise he's the murderer.

Visual Ideas: One of the greatest shots in Hitch's career comes at the end when the camera pans over the lobby of the Grand Hotel, into the tea-room where a band is playing and, from 145 feet zooms in to 4 inches from the drummer, whose eyes then start to twitch, revealing him to be the murderer. At the same time, the band plays a song about the Drummer Man - the person Erica and Will are looking for - which includes the lyric "I'm right here." Awe-inspiring. It was shot on Pinewood's biggest sound stage and took two days to get in the camera. The crane shot was repeated to less effect in *Notorious*.

Audio Ideas: A jazz band plays over the titles, which only becomes significant at the end, because the murderer is a drummer with a jazz band. Opens with a black screen and a man shouting, "Christine," which gets your attention. When women discover Christine's body on the beach, they scream but Hitch cuts to the cries of seagulls.

Subtext: The children act like adults, and the adults act like children. At the party the children are behaved and formal whilst the adults wear silly hats and play games. At Erica's home the children are formal using adult words. When Erica and Robert stop at a garage a boy fills the car whilst his dad has his mouth full eating. Conversely, at Tom's Hat the adults start a fight, the two policemen with Erica act like children and the two witnesses at the beach begin to cry when Robert says they are lying.

Recurring Ideas: Birds (The cry of seagulls represents a scream, rooks pecking at eyes are referred to over dinner); Eyes (The villain's eyes twitch, Robert steals glasses to escape, playing Blindman's Bluff at the children's party, reference to rooks pecking at eyes); Changing Identities (Christine is an actress, the murderer's band is in blackface make-up, Robert is a screenwriter and puts on his solicitor's glasses to escape, Will the tramp dresses in posh clothes to get into the Grand Hotel); The Wrong Man/The Man On The Run; The Fatal Flaw (The twitching eyes).

The Walk-On: Outside the courts, Hitch is a big press photographer with a tiny camera.

The Verdict: A charming film and one of Hitch's sweetest. It is both fun and exciting. 4/5

The Lady Vanishes (1938)

Cast: Margaret Lockwood (Iris Henderson), Michael Redgrave (Gilbert Redman), Paul Lukas (Dr Hartz), Dame May Whitty (Miss Froy), Cecil Parker (Eric Todhunter), Linden Travers ('Mrs' Margaret Todhunter), Naunton Wayne (Caldicott), Basil Radford (Charters), Mary Clare (Baroness), Googie Withers (Blanche), Phillip Leaver (Signor Doppo), Catherine Lacey (The Nun)

Crew: Director Alfred Hitchcock, Screenplay Sidney Gilliat & Frank Launder, Novel *The Wheel Spins* Ethel Lina White, Producer Edward Black, Original Music Louis Levy & Cecil Milner, Cinematographer Jack E Cox, Film Editing R E Dearing

Blonde Virgin: Margaret Lockwood, only she's not blonde, and probably no virgin either.

The MacGuffin: Miss Froy.

Story: A group of people are in a hotel waiting for the next train: Charters & Caldicott (two silly-ass Englishmen who talk of Cricket and nothing else); Miss Froy (an old governess who is leaving the country after six years); Iris Henderson (a rich playgirl on her way home to get married); and Gilbert Redman (a whimsical collector of folk songs who keeps the rest of the hotel awake with loud music and dancing). Miss Froy tries to remember the song being sung below her window, unaware that the serenader is strangled. As they board the train the next day, Iris is hit on the head by a falling flowerpot intended for Miss Froy. Dizzy, Iris is helped by Miss Froy, has tea with her and then falls asleep. When she wakes, Miss Froy is missing and no one remembers her (Caldicott doesn't want Iris to stop the train so that he'd miss the cricket match, an English lawyer on an illicit romantic interlude doesn't want to get involved). Confused, Iris searches the train and gets help from Gilbert and Dr Hartz, the latter explaining that a bump on the head can cause hallucinations. Iris tries to convince them there is a conspiracy and eventually persuades Gilbert when he sees a discarded packet of Miss Froy's herbal tea. They go to the boxcar to see if Miss Froy is hidden there and find her broken glasses - a fight ensues with the Italian magician The Great Doppo, who disappears with the evidence. Dr Hartz's patient is accompanied by a deaf and dumb nun whom Iris and Gilbert suspect because she wears high heels. They find out that the bandaged patient is Miss Froy and confide their discovery to Hartz, whom we find out is the villain. Hartz tries to drug our heroes but the nun changes sides, they free Miss Froy and put another spy in her place. Hartz uncouples the carriage and directs it to a forest where he demands Miss Froy and a gunfight ensues. Miss Froy reveals to Gilbert that he must remember a folk tune and get it to England because it contains some secret code. Some of the English are shot and die, Miss Froy makes a run for it and Gilbert and Charters get the train out of there. Iris and Gilbert declare their love for each other on their way back to England but Gilbert forgets the tune, and we end on a nice tracking shot going into the foreign office, hearing the piano play the tune and seeing Miss Froy playing it.

Visual Ideas: Vanishing (The serenader is killed. Just before Miss Froy vanishes, the Italian in the carriage does a magic trick with his hands. He is The Great Doppo, a stage magician whose best trick is 'the vanishing lady.' There are many vanishings in the storage car using his props. Finally, at the shoot-out, Miss Froy vanishes herself into the forest); Waking Up/Sleeping (Only the heroes sleep. The villains are always awake, dangerous, taking advantage of sleep. At the beginning in the hotel, there are many scenes with people going to bed, and Iris spends most of the film going asleep/fainting and waking up to chaos, the villains having done their dirty work. Both Gilbert and Iris pretend to be asleep when they are not drugged by Dr Hartz).

Audio Ideas: Music (Miss Froy talks about her love of music, Gilbert collects folk songs for a book. Music brings Gilbert and Iris together. The 'Colonel Bogey' is whistled, and mention is made of the 'Hungarian Rhapsody.' We find out that the tune Miss Froy was learning at the beginning is a code which contains a secret clause of a pact between two countries, and she entrusts Gilbert with remembering it. Gilbert hums the tune on the journey home, but when he kisses Iris, he can only remember 'The Wedding March.' Ironic, because the reason for his trip was to bring back music); Englishness (Constant references to the English abroad especially through the hilarious Charters & Caldicott, including Herriman's Herbal Tea, Sugar, Cricket, Stiff Upper Lip and the ultimate in Englishness when the dining car carriage is uncoupled it is teatime so all the English are in the dining car).

Subtext: The key to this movie is the title. Physically, Miss Froy vanishes, but emotionally the lady in Iris vanishes too, and remains lost. At the beginning, Iris is a bit stuck up but by the end, after she has been rejected by everybody on board, and her ladylike virtues have been stripped, her true character is revealed and she falls in love.

Recurring Ideas. The Switch (The nun is supposed to be deaf and dumb, then she is revealed to be a spy for the villains, but turns traitor when she finds out they intend to kill an Englishwoman. She puts her life at risk and finally gives her life to save the others); The Cultured Villain (Dr Hartz of Prague is a respected brain surgeon who has worked on British heads of state, an educated man, who seems to be on Iris and Gilbert's side, but isn't. When they escape, he is still a nice villain because he says, "Jolly good luck to them."); The Train (Hitch likes trains, doesn't he?); Birds (Pigeons are part of The Great Doppo's magic act); The Woman's Point Of View (Iris - an iris is part of the eye, which is for looking, for shedding light on things - is the central character and virtually everything is seen through her eyes).

The Walk-On: Hitch appears in a London railway station right at the end - he's not obvious.

The Verdict: Like a perfectly baked soufflé, this light concoction is flimsy but tasty. 5/5

Jamaica Inn (1939)

Cast: Charles Laughton (Sir Humphrey Pengallan), Leslie Banks (Joss Merlyn), Emlyn Williams (Harr), Robert Newton (Jim Trehearne), Marie Ney (Patience), Wylie Watson (Salvation), Maureen O'Hara (Mary Yelland)

Crew: Director Alfred Hitchcock, Adaptation Alma Reville, Dialogue Sidney Gilliat, Additional Dialogue Joan Harrison & J B Priestley, Novel Daphne Du Maurier, Producers Charles Laughton & Erich Pommer, Original Music Eric Fenby, Cinematographers Bernard Knowles & Harry Stradling Sr., Film Editing Robert Hamer, Special Effects Harry Watts

Story: Mary Yelland, a young Irish girl, goes to live in Cornwall with her Aunt Patience and Uncle Joss Merlyn, who run a tavern. This tavern is the haunt of wreckers, who find out where ships are, lure them to the rocky coast and make a profit from the remains. They are immune from prosecution because their leader is the local Justice of the Peace, Sir Humphrey Pengallan.

The Verdict: Although meaningless rubbish, it does manage to be fun, and helped launch the hundreds of costume dramas that haunted English films throughout the 1940s and 1950s. 2/5

3. Lost In America (1940-1947)

In the late 1930s, although many films were being made in Britain, they were made inefficiently and the losses incurred led to the closure of several studios. Hitchcock was making success after success and realised that the only way he could make a lot of money was to move to America. He canvassed the studios in Hollywood with little success. Only David O Selznick seemed interested so, after some haggling, Hitch signed a 4-picture deal with him on 14 July 1938 in New York. Hitch would get $40,000 a picture, plus a generous weekly salary when he wasn't filming. Hitch returned to England to film his outstanding commitment, *Jamaica Inn*, and then moved to America. The relationship with Selznick began with the successful *Rebecca*, but Hitch soon found himself hired out by Selznick to other companies. Hitch was most displeased to find out how much of a profit Selznick was making from this process, although it must be said his best films of this period (*Shadow Of A Doubt*, *Notorious*) were made away from Selznick.

Rebecca (1940)

Cast: Laurence Olivier (George Fortescu Maximillian 'Maxim' de Winter), Joan Fontaine (The Second Mrs de Winter), George Sanders (Jack Favell), Judith Anderson (Mrs Danvers), Gladys Cooper (Beatrice Lacy), Nigel Bruce (Major Giles Lacy), C Aubrey Smith (Colonel Julyan), Leo G Carroll (Dr Baker)

Crew: Director Alfred Hitchcock, Adaptation Philip MacDonald & Michael Hogan, Screenplay Robert E Sherwood & Joan Harrison, Novel Daphne Du Maurier, Producer David O Selznick, Original Music Franz Waxman, Cinematographer George Barnes, Film Editing W Donn Hayes & Hal C Kern

Blonde Virgin: Joan Fontaine, The Second Mrs de Winter.

The MacGuffin: The First Mrs de Winter.

Story: Fontaine's character (she is never named), the paid companion of Mrs Edythe Van Hopper, falls in love with rich Maxim de Winter whilst in Monte Carlo. She is a sweet, gentle, innocent lost soul. He is a brooding older man with a dark secret - they first meet in the opening scene when he is standing on the edge of a cliff, looking as though he is about to jump and she shouts to stop him. It is a whirlwind romance, punctuated by his occasional temper-tantrums - he seems very cold and distant at times. It seems that his wife, Rebecca, died under tragic circumstances which still haunt Maxim. Fontaine and Maxim wed. After the honeymoon, the couple go to Manderley in Cornwall, a giant house, driving in the light, then it suddenly becomes dark and the rain pours. Completely out of her depth, Mrs de Winter meets the servants and the frosty housekeeper Mrs Danvers, not knowing what to do or say. The house is full of references to Rebecca: personalised napkins, address books, paper, etc. Mrs Danvers, who loved Rebecca, keeps her memory alive and exerts her authority over the new Mrs de Winter, remaking her into the image of Rebecca. She introduces Fontaine to Rebecca's room, a dark place full of sensuality (putting a fur coat to her cheek) and sexuality (the see-through nightdress). When Fontaine dresses as Rebecca, Maxim rejects her. Fontaine in tears, Mrs Danvers whispers persuasive reasons for Fontaine to kill herself. Fireworks signalling a ship in distress save Fontaine from jumping. Rebecca's sunken boat is found with Rebecca's body inside it. Maxim reveals he hated Rebecca, that she was pregnant with Favell's child, that she collapsed and died in front of him so he put her in their boat and sunk it. During the inquest Favell tries to blackmail Maxim with a letter, but an investigation reveals that Rebecca died of cancer. Rebecca was evil, spiteful, malignant and beautiful with it. Returning to Manderley in the dark, Maxim notices it is light because Manderley is burning, aflame, torched by Mrs Danvers who could not live with her misplaced love for Rebecca.

Visual Ideas: A close-up of Rebecca's monogrammed napkin tracks out to show a tiny Fontaine in a giant room. There are many tracks and pans through the house, giving it an eerie atmosphere, but few of Hitchcock's usual funny or ironic set pieces. Also, perversely, in two scenes Hitch ditches the luscious set and opts for a black screen with only the eyes or mouth in a rectangle of light - when Max and Fontaine are watching their honeymoon on film, and when Mrs Danvers is persuading Fontaine to commit suicide - scenes which concentrate on emotional issues. Mrs Danvers herself is inhuman, almost like Eisenstein's Ivan the Terrible, completely in black, a staring, immobile face, never seen walking, always appearing when you least expect her.

Audio Ideas: This is the first real use of signature music in Hitchcock's films, where the characters have their own themes. Franz Waxman creates an atmosphere with his music which perfectly complements the images, and forever reminds us that Rebecca haunts Manderley.

Subtext: The central character does not have a name other than Mrs de Winter, and is constantly in competition with the named, but never seen,

Rebecca. In order to reclaim her place in the film, the second Mrs de Winter thinks that she must become Rebecca, not realising she must become herself. The house and Mrs Danvers are still part of Rebecca, and it is only when they are burned down, and all traces of Rebecca are removed, that the couple can carry on with their lives. Each of the characters have their own view of Rebecca (much like the later *Citizen Kane* (1941, director Orson Welles) and *Laura* (1944, director Otto Preminger)), and this leads to the central conflict in the film.

Recurring Ideas: Water (It starts at the sea, Rebecca died in the sea, it rains all the time (even inside you see the shadow of rainwater flowing down the walls as though the very house is crying), and the second Mrs de Winter cries all the time); Woman's Point Of View (Taken entirely from Mrs de Winter's point of view, with voice-over at the beginning); The Cultured Villain (Jack Favell is charming and roguish and winning, but was Rebecca's lover. He turns to blackmail and accusations of murder); The Shock Twist (For half the movie we believe Maxim to be still in love with Rebecca, but we are shocked to find out he has always hated her); The Wrong Woman (Fontaine's character thinks that she is not right for Maxim, and thinks she should become Rebecca, but only finds out towards the end that Maxim hates Rebecca - so she was trying to become the wrong woman); Hiding Mistakes (Just as Stevie in *Sabotage* hides the plate he broke in a kitchen drawer, Fontaine hides the statue she breaks in a drawer).

The Walk-On: As George Sanders makes a call in a phone booth, Hitch walks by, but his face is hidden, so not much of a walk-on.

And Another Thing: Of all Hitchcock's films, this is still the most popular to general audiences, mainly because of its appeal to women. It established Hitch in America and made him 'hot' in today's parlance. It even got a Best Picture Oscar, although Selznick received that as Producer, and Cinematographer George Barnes got an Oscar too. Hitch never received an Oscar for Best Director although he was nominated five times.

The Verdict: Brooding, gothic, the atmosphere is only spoilt by too much exposition and running around at the end without Fontaine, who's great. 4/5

Foreign Correspondent (1940)

Cast: Joel McCrea (Johnny Jones/Huntley Haverstock), Laraine Day (Carol Fisher), Herbert Marshall (Stephen Fisher), George Sanders (Scott ffolliott), Albert Bassermann (Van Meer), Robert Benchley (Stebbins), Edmund Gwenn (Rowley), Eduardo Ciannelli (Mr Krug), Harry Davenport (Mr Powers)

Crew: Director Alfred Hitchcock, Screenplay Robert Benchley & Charles Bennett & Harold Clurman & Joan Harrison & Ben Hecht & James Hilton & John Howard Lawson & John Lee Mahin & Richard Maibaum & Budd Schulberg, Producer Walter Wanger, Original Music Alfred Newman, Cinematographer Rudolph Maté, Film Editing Dorothy Spencer, Camera Operator Burnett Guffey, Special Production Effects William Cameron Menzies

Blonde Virgin: Laraine Day, although she's a brunette.

The MacGuffin: Clause 27.

Story: Troublesome reporter Johnny Jones goes to Europe to interview Van Meer in London, at a luncheon organised by the Universal Peace Party, to find out whether he thinks war is going to be declared. Jones questions Van Meer, but he is too elusive, so Jones concentrates on wooing Carol Fisher, daughter of Stephen Fisher, leader of the Universal Peace Party. At a peace conference in Amsterdam, Van Meer is assassinated in front of Jones. A car chase ensues leading Jones to windmills, where he discovers that Van Meer is alive - a double has been killed - and the villains want Clause 27, a secret clause to a peace treaty which Van Meer memorised. Jones is then hunted by villains, which brings him and Carol together. They escape to London, to her father, only for Jones to find out that Stephen Fisher is the master villain and his organisation is a front. (Jones cannot tell Carol this.) Jones is taken to the top of a cathedral tower to have an accident, only it is affable assassin Rowley who falls to his death. Scott ffolliott, a fellow newspaperman - a slightly sinister observer of a lot of the events - works with Jones to get Van Meer. Ffolliott pretends that Carol has been kidnapped (actually, she has gone away with Jones) and tries to blackmail Fisher into giving away Van Meer's whereabouts, but the plan fails when Carol returns too soon. ffolliott tracks down Van Meer, who is being systematically interrogated. In a fight, ffolliott escapes through a window and falls down through an awning, whilst Fisher escapes with Carol onto a plane to America as war is declared. "It would be nice to live in the clouds," Carol says in the plane. She finds out that her father is a spy, that he works for war, rather

44

than against it. Fisher says that he loves her, that he is ashamed of the way he deceived her. They are attacked by a German ship, are hit and crash. People die, but some survive on the wing of the plane. It is sinking under the weight of the people so Fisher quietly slips off the wing. They are picked up by an American boat and Jones broadcasts to America, from London, warning of the destruction to come, giving America a wake up call.

Visual Ideas: Van Meer's assassination starts with a long pan of the street, zoom into Jones, then Van Meer up the steps, being shot by a photographer, and the assassin escaping through a sea of umbrellas. We see the umbrellas from the top – a shot copied by many other directors. When Clause 27 is being beaten out of Van Meer, we see the reactions of the others in the room, which makes the beating even worse. In one continuous shot we go closer and then into the flying plane to focus on Carol and her father. The plane crash is brilliantly done - we stay inside all the time. We are in the cockpit when they hit the water, and we see the water come through the window - there's no cut. Sinking, the water level rises, very claustrophobic, frightening.

Recurring Ideas: Hats (Jones needs a hat when he leaves for England but children steal it. He leaves a hat in a taxi. In Amsterdam his hat blows off and he runs after it which leads to the discovery of the windmill. In the cathedral tower a boy's hat blows off and at the end Jones says that he's talking through his hat); Birds (When we first meet Van Meer he talks about birds to deflect talk away from politics. In the windmill Van Meer looks at the hidden Jones and the villains turn around to see a bird in his place (Jones has flown). When Van Meer is interrogated he says, "You'll never conquer them, the little people who give crumbs to birds"); The Cultured Villain (Stephen Fisher is a respected man in international politics and, unusually, loves his daughter more than he loves his country, which makes him sympathetic. Eventually, he gives up his life for her); Towers (The opening shot is the top of a New York skyscraper. The windmills. The Cathedral tower); In The Middle Of Nowhere (After the car chase, Jones is left in the bushes, alone, a plane buzzing overhead, with just the creaking of the windmills for company - just like *North By Northwest*).

The Walk-On: Just before Jones meets Van Meer, Hitch is reading a newspaper on the street.

And Another Thing: The original ending was weak, so Ben Hecht was called in to write the radio commentator under fire scene, which was pure propaganda. As it happened it was prophetic - filmed on 5 July 1940, the first bombs started dropping on London just 5 days later.

The Verdict: Although Jones loses centre stage towards the end - he is consistently out-dialogued by Edmund Gwenn as Rowley, Herbert Marshall as Fisher and George Sanders as ffolliott - the set pieces are excellent and the pace relentless. This is a BIG picture, not a B-picture, as suggested by François Truffaut. 4/5

Mr & Mrs Smith (1941)

Cast: Carole Lombard (Ann Krausheimer Smith), Robert Montgomery (David Smith), Gene Raymond (Jeff Custer), Jack Carson (Chuck Benson)

Crew: Director Alfred Hitchcock, Screenplay Norman Krasna, Producer Harry E Edington, Original Music Edward Ward, Cinematographer Harry Stradling Sr., Film Editing William Hamilton

Blonde Virgin: Carole Lombard.

The MacGuffin: Sex.

Story: A couple who quarrel a lot discover that they are not legally married. The remainder of the film charts the quarrel-to-end-all-quarrels as Mr Smith tries to persuade Miss Krausheimer that he loves her. I don't think I need to explain what happens in the end.

The Verdict: A romantic comedy which has some moments of both romance and comedy, but not in sufficient amounts to retain interest for 95 minutes. 1/5

Suspicion (1941)

Cast: Cary Grant (Johnnie Aysgarth), Joan Fontaine (Lina McLaidlaw Aysgarth), Cedric Hardwicke (General McLaidlaw), Nigel Bruce (Beaky), Dame May Whitty (Mrs McLaidlaw), Isabel Jeans (Mrs Newsham), Leo G Carroll (Captain Melbeck)

Crew: Director & Producer Alfred Hitchcock, Screenplay Samson Raphaelson & Joan Harrison & Alma Reville, Novel *Before The Fact* Francis Iles, Original Music Franz Waxman, Cinematographer Harry Stradling Sr., Film Editing William Hamilton

Blonde Virgin: Joan Fontaine.

The MacGuffin: Trust.

Story: Lina and Johnnie meet on a train, and they are attracted to each other despite initial impressions. She is spinsterish to him, and he is childish to her. At a hunt, he sees her control a wild horse, sees her radiant smile and sees her in a completely new light. He engineers a meeting and it ends with a kiss. When he disappears, Lina searches for him but she cannot make contact. Depressed, she is delighted when they meet at the hunt ball and he proposes to her that night. A whirlwind romance ends with an elopement, a honeymoon in Europe and a new house. When Lina finds out that it's all paid for on borrowed money, she says that Johnnie must get a job, which he does. Johnnie's betting results in mounting debts, so he does a rash thing - he sells two of Lina's precious chairs, bets the money on a horse and wins £2,000. After the celebrations, Lina accidentally finds out that Johnnie is no longer at work, that he was sacked, and that he stole £2,000 which he is being given time to replace. In Lina's mind, Johnnie is now a desperate character looking for money and will do anything to get it. When Johnnie suggests a cliff-side property development deal with Beaky, their best friend, and Lina thinks that Johnnie is thinking of killing Beaky for the money, she faints. When she wakes up, she finds tyre tracks on the edge of the cliff. Fearing the worse, she returns to find Johnnie has actually saved Beaky's life. Soon after, when Beaky dies in Paris, she suspects Johnnie, who went missing. Next Lina finds he has arranged a life insurance policy without telling her and, at dinner with a mystery writer, when Johnnie asks about an undetectable poison Lina fears for her life. Faint, in bed, Johnnie fetches Lina a glass of milk. Convinced it contains poison, the next morning Lina packs to leave. Driving Lina to her mothers, Johnnie saves her from falling out of the car, and she finds out the truth - Johnnie was contemplating suicide, but now he has decided to go to jail. Lina decides to stay with Johnnie through the bad times.

Visual Ideas: Like some other Hitch movies, this starts with a black screen with dialogue. When Lina and Johnnie slowly kiss after the Hunt Ball, the camera swirls around them à la *Vertigo* - it IS a whirlwind romance, after all. When Lina fears Beaky is dead by Johnnie's hand, the shadows look like a giant web. She moves in darkness, and is dark herself, but when she sees Beaky alive both she and her surroundings become light. The film is seen from Lina's point of view, so the appearance of things changes depending on her state of mind. Lina 'saw' Beaky's death by looking at the photo of the cliff-side land and seeing one figure push another off the cliff, Beaky screaming (although laughing in person), and him falling into the waves. When Johnnie is suspect in Lina's eyes, he is dark and serious. When he is bringing milk for her, which Lina thinks is poisoned, we follow him out of the kitchen and up the stairs, a luminous glass of milk on a tray - Hitch had actually put a light bulb in it! The final scene in the fast car gives us the alienating view of Johnnie seen from the side, without eye contact, ignoring both us and Lina.

Audio Ideas: Composer Franz Waxman repeatedly uses the waltz from the hunt ball (their tune) in an ironic context, both to confirm their love, and when played slightly off-key, to show that Lina doubts Johnnie's love for her.

Subtext: This is a story about people who cannot help but to destroy themselves. Lina cannot believe that anyone in their right mind could love her - she first kisses Johnnie because she overhears her parents say that she will never find a man - and so when she is married to Johnnie she finds reasons for him to be with her other than for love i.e. money. Johnnie is driven to take money and spend it, and the more money he spends the more he has to steal. Johnnie is compelled to do this - it is not for his own gain, but because he wants to buy Lina and his friends presents. He even buys himself a pet, just like a child. This penchant for self-destruction is best illustrated by their friend Beaky, who knows Brandy is poison to him but continues to drink it. In the end, Beaky is destroyed by his compulsion, Lina is changed by Johnnie's actions and comes to realise that he loves her, and Johnnie makes the decision to change himself. As Johnnie says at the end, "People don't change overnight."

Recurring Ideas: Money; Children (When we first see Lina she is reading a book on child psychology. Johnnie acts childishly all the time - like the time he plays with Lina's hair - with no sense of responsibility. When Lina finds out that he borrowed the money for their honeymoon she tells him "You're a baby." Beaky acts like a child by going to the corner of the room as a punishment); The Wrong Man (Unusually for Hitch, instead of seeing things from the accused's point of view, we see it from the accuser's. In this case, Johnnie is guilty, but not of murder); Train; Birds (Err, their best friend is called Beaky).

The Original Ending: Hitch filmed Johnnie killing Lina at the end instead of saving her, but it previewed badly so it was changed.

And Another Thing: Hitch made Joan Fontaine a major star with *Rebecca*, and for her performance in *Suspicion* she won an Oscar.

The Verdict: Despite all the problems making the film, especially coming up with a suitable ending, this still ranks as a classy piece of film-making. Hitchcock psychology is rampant. Cary Grant playing a villain?! Who would have believed it? 4/5

Saboteur (1942)

Cast: Priscilla Lane (Patricia Martin), Robert Cummings (Barry Kane), Otto Kruger (Charles Tobin), Alan Baxter (Mr Freeman), Clem Bevans (Neilson), Norman Lloyd (Fry), Alma Kruger (Mrs Sutton), Vaughan Glaser (Mr Miller), Dorothy Peterson (Mrs Mason), Billy Curtis (Midget)

Crew: Director & Story Alfred Hitchcock, Screenplay Peter Viertel & Joan Harrison & Dorothy Parker, Producers Frank Lloyd & Jack H Skirball, Original Music Frank Skinner, Cinematographer Joseph A Valentine, Film Editing Otto Ludwig

Blonde Virgin: Priscilla Lane.

The MacGuffin: Find Fry.

Story: Barry Kane and his friend Mason work at an aircraft factory and bump into a guy who drops his stuff all over the floor. Kane helps pick up the guy's letters, and sees he's called Fry. The alarms go off, the sprinklers aren't working and Fry hands an extinguisher to Kane, who hands it to Mason. Mason goes up in flames - the extinguisher had been filled with gasoline. Kane is accused of sabotage, since nobody else saw Fry, and goes on the run. Remembering the address on the letters, Kane goes to Springville via a friendly truck driver. At the Deep Springs Ranch, he meets the friendly Mr Tobin, who denies knowing Fry. It's an informal talk and, as Tobin rings his neighbour, his little girl gets letters from Tobin's jacket, one of which is from Fry saying he will be at Soda City. Tobin sees this, Kane makes his escape using the girl as a shield, is lassoed by the cowhands and delivered to the police. The handcuffed Kane escapes by jumping off a bridge into a river, and finds respite in the cabin of a blind musician, who believes Kane to be innocent. The musician asks his niece Patricia to take Kane to the local blacksmith to remove the handcuffs but she is on the way to the police, so Kane takes over the car and severs the handcuffs with the car's fan, causing the car to break down. They hitch a ride with the circus freaks (a brilliant scene written by Dorothy Parker). From that moment Patricia and Kane are together. In Soda City, a ghost town by the Boulder Dam, Kane meets Mr Freeman (a spy) and pretends to be one of them. Whilst he goes to New York with them, Patricia goes to the police. The policeman is also a spy, so Patricia and Kane end up together in Mrs Sutton's house in New York, in the presence of mastermind Tobin, during a charity ball. Patricia and Kane escape to the ball, and they approach people there, but nobody believes they are among spies, and the spies (servants included) are covering all the exits. Patricia is kidnapped and Kane stands up to talk, but a hidden gun is trained on him, so he starts the charity auction and is led away to Tobin. Patricia and Kane are held separately and escape under their own steam (Patricia by throwing a note out of a skyscraper, Kane by setting off the sprinklers with a match). Kane goes to the Brooklyn shipyard to prevent a ship from being bombed at its launch - he sees Fry in the back of a newsreel van, they fight, the bomb goes off, but only after the ship is launched. Kane is caught by the spies, who return to the Rockefeller Center where the police are waiting (thanks to Patricia). Fry gets out through the cinema, and is followed by Patricia while Kane is held for questioning by the FBI. Fry goes to the Statue of Liberty to hide. Patricia follows and phones the FBI, but she has to keep Fry there and starts talking to him. The FBI arrives, Fry goes up to the flame, Kane goes after him, Fry hangs over the edge, Kane tries to save him by holding Fry's sleeve, but the sleeve unravels and Fry falls.

Visual Ideas: Over the credits the shadow of a walking man gradually gets bigger and bigger, just like when the plant is on fire the smoke gets bigger and bigger. When Kane is on the run, from the truck he sees a slogan on a billboard which reads: 'You Are Being Followed.' Later, when Patricia is driving him to the police another billboard slogan says: 'She'll Never Let You Down.' In the cinema, there are giant faces on the screen with the tiny figure of Fry in shadow (literally 'small fry').

Audio Ideas: When Fry and Kane are struggling at the shipyard, there is no sound - they fight in silence. Atop the Statue of Liberty, there is no sound except the wind and the occasional ship's horn. Hitch often used silence, or just low-key location sound to heighten the tension.

Subtext: This is a propaganda film against the American fifth columnists, which uses the imagery of fire and water to explain the dilemma. The fifth columnists let fire and water go out of control (burning the aircraft plant, blowing up the shipyard), whilst the heroes try to control it. The ultimate symbol of this is the flame on the Statue of Liberty surrounded by water, which is where the film ends. Also, with Fry hiding inside the statue, the symbolism is, of course, that spies hide under the cloak of liberty. This fight is everlasting - so Tobin is not caught at the end.

Recurring Ideas: Fire (Opening shot of the aircraft plant workers lighting cigarettes on their break, the plant is burned down, a truck driver says "Go ahead and give me the hot news," a policeman says to a captured Kane "You'll have time to burn," putting a log on the fire, the stove with the radio in it, the flame on the Statue of Liberty); Not Fire (When Kane visits Mason's mother she has four candles in front of her but none of them are lit); Water (Extinguishers in plant (do not work) and in truck (works), sprinkler systems in plant (do not work) and at Mrs Sutton's house (works), Kane jumps into a river to escape from the police, it rains as he gets to the blind musician's cabin, the Boulder Dam, an admiral takes over the auction, the Brooklyn shipyard is blown up); The Wrong Man/Man On The Run (Kane runs across America from Los Angeles to New York); Handcuffs; Cinema Screen (Absolutely brilliant scene where Fry, on the run, goes through a cinema full of laughing people, and the dialogue/gunplay on screen ironically matches the 'real-life' situation. "Run, he'll kill you." etc. People get shot); The Cultured Villain (Tobin is seen playing with his baby granddaughter, hobnobbing with society and finally escapes to the Caribbean until the war blows over); The Public Place (The Charity Ball, Cinema, the Statue of Liberty); The Family Of Spies (As well as seeing Tobin's family, Freeman talks about raising his children and a spy who is darning his sock comments that he hopes things are over soon so that he can take his kid sister to the Philharmonic).

The Walk-On: Apparently, Hitch is at a news-stand but it's not obvious. I didn't see him!

The Verdict: Most people put down this film, including Hitch, because it doesn't have such big stars, and the sets aren't very lavish and other such nonsense, but I completely disagree with these notions. The script is very witty, the central characters have a homely, everyman feeling to them, and the action moves so quickly you don't have time to look at the decor. 4/5

Shadow Of A Doubt (1943)

Cast: Teresa Wright (Young Charlie Newton), Joseph Cotten (Charlie Oakley), Macdonald Carey (Jack Graham), Henry Travers (Joseph Newton), Patricia Collinge (Emma Newton), Hume Cronyn (Herbie Hawkins), Wallace Ford (Fred Saunders), Edna Mae Wonacott (Ann Newton), Charles Bates (Roger Newton)

Crew: Director Alfred Hitchcock, Screenplay Thornton Wilder & Sally Benson & Alma Reville, Story Gordon McDonell, Producer Jack H Skirball, Original Music Dimitri Tiomkin, Cinematographer Joseph A Valentine, Film Editing Milton Carruth

Blonde Virgin: Teresa Wright is not blonde but she gives every indication of being a virgin and I, for one, believe her.

The MacGuffin: Proof of Uncle Charlie's guilt.

Story: In a decaying city, Uncle Charlie is being pursued by two men, so he decides to visit his sister Emma in Santa Rosa. Charlie, his niece, is bored with life, complaining that the family is in a rut, that nothing happens, so she decides to telegraph her Uncle Charlie to come visit. Everything is fine until two men come to interview the family for a national survey. As Charlie falls for one of the men (they are detectives), she begins to doubt her Uncle Charlie is as nice as he seems. When she realises that he is the Merry Widow murderer, she agrees to get him out of town to save distressing her mother too much. Another man is killed and believed to be the murderer, so the detectives go. Charlie knows her uncle is the real killer, and he knows she knows so Uncle Charlie twice attempts to kill his niece. In retaliation, Charlie finds the ring - evidence that her Uncle Charlie is the killer. As Uncle Charlie leaves town, he tries to kill her, but he falls out of the train instead. Charlie vows to keep her uncle's murders a secret, to protect her mother.

Visual Ideas: When Uncle Charlie eludes the two men following him they are small, like ants, to him. To show a connection between Charlie and her uncle, our introduction to them is when they are lying in bed fully clothed, thinking - Uncle Charlie in Philadelphia, Charlie in Santa Rosa. As the steam train pulls into the station, delivering Uncle Charlie, the incredibly black smoke from the train covers the station in darkness.

Audio Ideas: The Merry Widow Waltz is heard over the opening credits, and throughout the film, which is appropriate for the Merry Widow murderer. In Hollywood it was convention for every word to be heard but in this film we have overlapping dialogue in the family scenes, something Robert Altman has since taken to heart in his ensemble films. When Uncle Charlie makes a speech about old women his voice becomes monotone, which gives him a sinister air.

Subtext: This is a modern-day battle between good and evil, expressed in the duality of Charlie and her Uncle Charlie. Hitch was raised on Victorian literature, like Robert Louis Stevenson's *The Strange Case Of Dr Jekyll And Mr Hyde* (1886) and Oscar Wilde's *The Picture Of Dorian Gray* (1891), where duality was a major theme. As Charlie grows up (she starts in a dress and ends in a suit) she has to decide whether to protect the world from evil, or to become evil herself.

Recurring Ideas: The Cultured Villain (Uncle Charlie is a perfect gentleman); Train (Uncle Charlie comes and goes on the train); The Double (Charlie and her Uncle Charlie are twins who share many similar thoughts and feelings - they are two sides of the same coin); Hats (Charlie complains that her mother went out wearing an old hat. When Uncle Charlie moves into Charlie's room Joseph tells him not to put his hat on the bed. "I don't believe in inviting trouble." Uncle Charlie throws his hat on the bed).

The Walk-On: Hitch is playing poker on the train, holding a full house. We don't see his face.

And Another Thing: Hitch's mother was ill whilst this film was being made, but he couldn't get to the UK. Hitch, normally secretive, began talking about his early life and lots of details made their way into the script. His tenderness towards her probably accounts for the benevolent mother figure, one of the last in his films. The mother is called Emma, the name of Hitch's mother. Uncle Charlie's bike accident as a child happened to Hitch. Hitch refused to drive a car, like Joseph. Ann reads *Ivanhoe*, a book Hitch knew by heart as a child. Herbie is mother-dominated and obsessed with murder.

The Verdict: A perfectly written, acted and directed film which is still fresh and packs a real punch. 5/5

Lifeboat (1944)

Cast: Tallulah Bankhead (Constance Porter), William Bendix (Gus Smith), Walter Slezak (Willy, the German Submarine Commander), Mary Anderson (Alice MacKenzie), John Hodiak (John Kovac), Henry Hull (Charles D 'Ritt' Rittenhouse), Heather Angel (Mrs Higgins), Hume Cronyn (Stanley Garrett), Canada Lee (George 'Joe' Spencer)

Crew: Director Alfred Hitchcock, Screenplay Jo Swerling & Ben Hecht, Story John Steinbeck, Producer Kenneth MacGowan, Original Music Hugo Friedhofer, Cinematographer Glen MacWilliams, Film Editing Dorothy Spencer

Blonde Virgin: Tallulah Bankhead, although she ain't no virgin.

The MacGuffin: Land.

Story: During wartime, a diverse group of people survive a U-boat attack and have to make it to Bermuda with no compass. The U-boat also blew up, and they have one of the crew on board. The businessman Rittenhouse elects himself boss and decides what everyone else does. Then Kovac becomes leader to show what it is like when a working man takes control. They start bickering amongst themselves. Then Willy, the German, takes control in a storm. He wins their confidence by cutting off Gus' bad leg and saving his life. Willy knows how to speak English, has a compass, and is strong enough to row them to a German supply ship while the others lie about doing nothing. Willy, who was the U-boat captain, kills Gus. When they discover Willy had water, and didn't give it to them, the rest kill him with Gus' spare shoe and throw him overboard. They start thinking for themselves, come across a German supply ship, which is then sunk. They pick up a German survivor, which begs the question: what is their attitude to the Germans now?

Visual Ideas: It's all set on a boat! There are some unusual pans and zooms, not normally seen in boat scenes. When they decide to follow a different direction, Willy is angry, which is shown by the sail going up and its shadow falling over Willy's face.

Subtext: Each of the characters lose the thing they love. The dancer his leg, the Communist his equality (he wants money from the Industrialist), the Industrialist his power, the mother her baby, the black man his voice, the reporter her camera and typewriter and bracelet. When they are stripped bare, what do they have left? It is a story about people being adrift, with no direction (literally) or cohesion. Only together can they defeat the German, who has a direction, confidence, energy and a sense of purpose. On the downside, they kill the German - there is a horrible price to pay. As Porter says, "The sins you do two by two, you pay for one by one."

Recurring Ideas: The Cultured Villain.

The Walk-On: As William Bendix reads a newspaper, Hitch is seen in before and after photos of a weight-reduction advert.

The Verdict: It may be propaganda, but it's great propaganda. 4/5

Bon Voyage (1944)

Cast: John Blythe, The Molière Players

Crew: Director Alfred Hitchcock, Screenplay Angus MacPhail & J O C Orton, Subject Arthur Calder-Marshall, Technical Advisor & Dialogue Claude Dauphin, Cinematographer Günther Krampf

Story: An RAF pilot in London is questioned by French Intelligence about his time in France. Dougall was on the run with a fellow prisoner of war, Godowski, making their way across France with the aid of the Resistance. When he finishes his tale, Dougall is told the true story, that Godowski was a spy.

The Verdict: Put together in trying circumstances to show the newly-liberated France the important role of the Resistance, there is only one moment of real suspense/horror when the Resistance girl is shot. This is okay but no great shakes. For the Hitchcock completist only. 2/5

Aventure Malgache (1944)

Alternative Title: Madagascar Landing (1944)
Cast: The Molière Players
Crew: Director Alfred Hitchcock, Cinematographer Günther Krampf
Story: An actor has trouble playing a part, so his fellow actor and former lawyer, Clarousse, tells him about Michel, the Chief of Police on Madagascar. Before the war, Clarousse tried to convict Michel on corruption charges but failed. When France was defeated by Germany, and Pétain agreed to the formation of the Vichy government, Clarousse pretended to change sides but led the Resistance and arranged for people to leave the island. Michel, of course, changed sides, remained in power, and did not trust Clarousse. A mistake was made and Clarousse was jailed - Michel tried all kinds of ways to trick information out of him but failed. Eventually, Clarousse was court-martialled and sentenced to death but his sentence was commuted to hard labour by Pétain himself, because Clarousse had fought at Verdun during The Great War. En route, Clarousse's ship was liberated, just as Madagascar was liberated by the English in May 1942. Michel tried to change sides again, but the English were not fooled, so Michel fled.

And Another Thing: Based on a true story, this film was not shown in France because of the sensitive subject matter. Many people supported the Vichy government, and this film suggested they were wrong to do so, which was judged to be the wrong message for France at that time.

The Verdict: Slow and boring, there are no discernible Hitchcock touches in this short film. 1/5

Spellbound (1945)

Cast: Ingrid Bergman (Dr Constance Peterson), Gregory Peck (Dr Edwardes/JB/John Ballantine), Michael Chekhov (Dr Brulov), Leo G Carroll (Dr Murchison), Rhonda Fleming (Mary Carmichael), John Emery (Dr Fleurot), Norman Lloyd (Garmes)
Crew: Director Alfred Hitchcock, Screenplay Ben Hecht, Novel *The House Of Dr Edwardes* Francis Beeding, Adaptation Angus MacPhail, Producer David O Selznick, Original Music Miklós Rózsa, Cinematographer George Barnes, Film Editing Hal C Kern & William H Ziegler, Dream Sequence Salvador Dalí, Psychiatric Advisor May E Romm
Blonde Virgin: Ingrid Bergman, who is actually blonde in this.
The MacGuffin: Peck's Memory.

Story: All-work-and-no-play Dr Peterson is suddenly in love with new head psychiatrist Dr Edwardes, who is there to replace Dr Murchison as the head of Green Manors, a psychiatric hospital. It soon becomes apparent that Dr Edwardes is mentally disturbed, and Peterson becomes more worried when she notices the signature on a signed edition of Edwardes' book is different to the one on a note to her. Edwardes says that he killed Edwardes and took his place. JB, as the mystery man is now called because of initials on his cigarette case, leaves and is pursued by the police. Peterson tracks JB down and discovers his hand was burnt, he had a skin graft not too long before and he was also a doctor. They go to Peterson's mentor, Dr Brulov, where they pretend to be a married couple. JB has an even worse attack - he wanders around with a cut-throat razor - and Peterson realises his attacks are triggered when he sees black lines on a white surface, like ski tracks on snow. JB tells them about his dream: He's playing cards in a place full of eyes, he draws the seven of clubs and a man with a beard says "that makes 21." A man falls off a sloping roof. A man without a face comes out with a wheel in his hand. JB is running into a valley being pursued by giant wings. Peterson and JB go to Gabriel Valley (wings = angel = Gabriel) and re-enact JB's skiing trip with Edwardes. As they ski down the slope, towards a cliff, JB remembers that as a child he caused the death of his brother, snaps out of his trance and saves Peterson from going over the cliff. Recovering his memory, he remembers he is John Ballantine and they tell the police everything. However Edwardes was shot, and Ballantine is convicted for murder. Back at Green Manors, Peterson is welcomed by Dr Murchison and says of Edwardes, "I knew him only slightly and never liked him" which means that he knew all along that Ballantine was not Edwardes. (Room of eyes = guards at hospital, Edwardes & Dr Murchison were at the 21 Club.) Dr Murchison is the murderer. He takes out his gun (wheel = revolver) and trains it on Peterson, but kills himself instead.

Visual Ideas: Black Lines On White (An inmate scratches a hand, fork marks on linen, the designs on a robe and bedsheet, the shadows in a bathroom); Milk (As JB drinks, we are seeing his view as the glass tips, through the bottom of the glass, and the screen goes white); Gun Hand (At the end, as Dr Murchison trains his gun on Peterson, we see his view of hand and gun following Peterson as she goes around the room, then she leaves and the gun turns towards us, fires, and there is a flash of red in this black and white film); Dream Sequence (It's designed by Salvador Dalí, so it's brilliant).

Recurring Ideas: The Wrong Man/Man On The Run; The Cultured Villain (Dr Murchison looks so kind); Milk (JB drinks milk, like Stebbins in *Foreign Correspondent*, and Lina in *Suspicion* and so many other characters); Psychological Explanation.

The Walk-On: Hitch is seen getting out of a crowded elevator.

The Verdict: Although Bergman is lovely, her scenes are far too long, the plot too flabby and Peck too bland. Hitch has a few interesting visual ideas, but there is no real excitement or tension. 2/5

Notorious (1946)

Cast: Cary Grant (T R Devlin), Ingrid Bergman (Alicia Huberman), Claude Rains (Alexander Sebastian), Louis Calhern (Paul Prescott), Leopoldine Konstantin (Madame Sebastian)

Crew: Director & Producer Alfred Hitchcock, Screenplay Ben Hecht, Original Music Roy Webb, Cinematographer Ted Tetzlaff, Film Editing Theron Warth, Second Unit Director Of Photography Gregg Toland

Blonde Virgin: Ingrid Bergman.

The MacGuffin: Uranium Ore.

Story: Alicia Huberman's father, a nazi, is tried and convicted of treason in Miami. Alicia is a tramp and a heavy drinker. She meets T R Devlin at a party, an American agent, who persuades her to spy for them in Rio de Janeiro. Waiting for their assignment, Alicia cleans up her act and they fall in love, only Devlin won't admit how he feels. One word from Devlin and she would not go on the assignment. They are told that Alicia is to meet Alexander Sebastian, an old friend of her father's who had a crush on her, and infiltrate his group. Alicia does better than that, she marries him. One of the group makes a fuss over a bottle of wine, so Alicia arranges for a party, steals Sebastian's key to the wine cellar and goes there with Devlin. Devlin discovers some ore in a bottle. Jealous Sebastian sees Devlin and Alicia kissing. Realising that Alicia is a spy and that his group will kill him if they find out, Sebastian and his mother decide to slowly poison Alicia, keeping her trapped in her room. Devlin comes to bring Alicia to hospital. Sebastian helps, wanting to go to the hospital to escape certain death from his group, but Devlin stops him getting in the car. Sebastian must return to his house where his group is waiting.

Visual Ideas: When Devlin is first introduced, he is a shadow who does not talk. When Alicia is drunk and driving fast, with hair in her eyes, we see her blurred point of view with strands across the screen. When Alicia wakes and sees Devlin walk towards her, the camera rotates until he is upside down to show her view. Incredible sequence: when Devlin and Alicia are in love, Hitch stays very close up to them talking, walking, phoning, kissing all the time, with their heads together, very intimate and erotic. From a large panorama of the party, Hitch pans across to Sebastian and Alicia, then zooms in on the key in her hand. The coffee full of poison is large in foreground, like the poisoned glasses in *The Lady Vanishes*. When Alicia realises she is being poisoned, there are zooms into faces and distorted swirling images which have since become the norm for such sequences. For such sunny places, Miami and Rio are filmed with incredible darkness.

Audio Ideas: The overlapping dialogue in dinner sequences, picking out words and phrases, is reminiscent of the knife scene in *Blackmail*.

Subtext: Alicia needs one word of love from Devlin and she is free from the nightmare that is her life. At the end, Devlin says, "I love you," and she escapes to freedom.

Recurring Ideas: The Cultured Villain; Milk (When Alicia wakes up from a hangover); Dominant Mother (Sebastian's mother is jealous of Alicia).

The Walk-On: Watch as Hitch drinks champagne at the party.

The Verdict: Like *Shadow Of A Doubt*, this is a meticulously scripted film which appeals to both the brain and the heart. 5/5

The Paradine Case (1947)

Cast: Gregory Peck (Anthony Keane), Ann Todd (Gay Keane), Charles Laughton (Judge Lord Horfield), Charles Coburn (Sir Simon Flaquer), Ethel Barrymore (Lady Sophie Horfield), Louis Jourdan (André Latour), Alida Valli (Mrs Maddalena Anna Paradine), Leo G Carroll (Council for the Prosecution)

Crew: Director Alfred Hitchcock, Screenplay James Bridie & Alma Reville & David O Selznick & Ben Hecht, Novel Robert Hichens, Producer David O Selznick, Original Music Franz Waxman, Cinematographer Lee Garmes, Film Editing John Faure & Hal C Kern

Blonde Virgin: Ann Todd.

The MacGuffin: The Truth.

Story: Young, beautiful, exotic Mrs Paradine is accused of poisoning her rich, blind, older husband, and top barrister Anthony Keane is brought in to defend her. It's obvious to everybody, including his wife, that the barrister has fallen for Mrs Paradine. He tries to prove that the valet, André Latour, poisoned his master after being dismissed. In the end,

Latour kills himself out of shame for failing his master, Mrs Paradine admits to the murder and says she loved Latour, Keane admits to the court that he made a mistake and his wife picks him up saying that he must put it behind him and carry on.

Visual Ideas: The beginning shows a series of pans to the left, almost like a spiral getting smaller, until we see Mrs Paradine. Similarly, the same spiral occurs when Keane is introduced. The photography is sometimes very harsh, with pure white light falling on the characters, but this documentary style is not used consistently, as in *The Wrong Man* and *I Confess* years later.

Subtext: This is all about love and trust, but ends up as a not-very-tense courtroom drama about people you don't know very well and don't care about.

Recurring Ideas: The Cultured Villainess (Hey, it's a woman this time!)

The Walk-On: Hitch is seen leaving a train station carrying a cello case.

The Verdict: Sometimes terribly, terribly English, this is a boring load of old tosh that is momentarily interesting when old codgers Laughton (as a lecherous Judge) or Coburn or Barrymore are on screen. 2/5

4. Breaking Free (1948-1949)

Hitch was fed up with kowtowing to the demands of David O Selznick and annoyed with being loaned out as a director-for-hire. He decided to form a company with his old friend Sidney Bernstein and produce his own films. Hitch knew that the only way he could make the films he wanted to make, with the minimum of interference from outsiders, was to produce. From this moment on, Hitch produced every film he ever worked on.

Rope (1948)

Cast: James Stewart (Rupert Cadell), John Dall (Shaw Brandon), Farley Granger (Philip), Sir Cedric Hardwicke (Mr Kentley), Constance Collier (Mrs Atwater), Douglas Dick (Kenneth Lawrence), Edith Evanson (Mrs Wilson, the Governess), Dick Hogan (David Kentley), Joan Chandler (Janet Walker)

Crew: Director Alfred Hitchcock, Screenplay Arthur Laurents & Ben Hecht, Play Patrick Hamilton, Adaptation Hume Cronyn, Producers Sidney Bernstein & Alfred Hitchcock, Original Music Leo F Forbstein, Additional Music Francis Poulenc (from 'Perpetual Movement No. 1'), Cinematographers William V Skall & Joseph A Valentine, Film Editing William H Ziegler

Blonde Virgin: David Kentley.

The MacGuffin: Shame.

Story: Philip and Brandon strangle David with a rope and put him in a chest. They have killed as an experiment. They prepare for the party they have arranged, and Brandon has an idea that will make our work of art a masterpiece" - he arranges for the food to be served on the chest, like some ceremonial alter. The guests arrive: David's father and his sister, David's girlfriend Janet and David's best friend Kenneth. Finally Rupert Cadell, who taught all four boys, and now a publisher of intellectual books, arrives - he is the only man Brandon looks up to. Everybody is concerned about the whereabouts of David. Brandon tries to reunite Janet and Kenneth, who were former lovers. The conversation turns to murder (it turns out that Philip is very proficient at strangling chickens), and Rupert explains that some people are superior to others and have the privilege to kill inferiors if they so wish. He says it in a lighthearted way but with conviction. Then things start going wrong: Janet and Kenneth argue with Brandon and virtually accuse him of kidnapping David; Rupert notices

Philip's agitation (especially when he sees the rope tied around books for David's father) and begins interrogating him. At the end of the party, Rupert puts on the wrong hat - it is David's hat. Brandon and Philip think they have got away with murder and prepare to dispose of David's body, but Rupert returns to find out the truth. A fight ensues over a gun, Rupert wins, fires three shots out of the window and waits for the police to come.

The Source Material: The play by Patrick Hamilton differs slightly from the film. In the play, Rupert is an old soldier who points out that when one gentleman murders another in a back alley for gain it is called murder and everybody wants revenge, yet when one generation murders another for no gain it is called war and everybody cheers. This is the basis for his position, which is clearly an intellectualisation of an emotional response to war. In the film, although his war record is mentioned, Rupert seems more like an intellectual without emotional experience who realises his position is wrong when he responds emotionally to David's death. To a certain extent, Rupert is to blame because he put these ideas into Brandon's head and encouraged him, although the act itself was carried out by Philip egged on by the dominant Brandon.

Visual Ideas: The whole movie is done in ten-minute takes (the maximum amount of film held in a film camera) and transitions from one take to the other are covered by the people walking into shot filling the screen. This gives us the impression that we are seeing what is happening in real time. This is the legend. However, there is one definite cut, when Brandon talks about Philip strangling chickens. Philip shouts and then we cut directly to Rupert's face.

Audio Ideas: Overlapping dialogue. The struggle for the gun is done in silence. At the end, all we hear is a siren getting louder and louder.

Recurring Ideas: The Cultured Villains (Two this time); Hats (Rupert discovers David's hat in the cupboard); Neon (Coloured lights make red, green and blue hues on the characters as emotions come to the boil).

The Walk-On: Hitch's famous profile drawing is seen as a flashing neon sign in the background.

And Another Thing: The play was based on the famous 1924 Leopold-Loeb case, the story of two homosexual law students in Chicago who murdered a 14-year-old boy for kicks to prove they were super intelligent and could get away with it. The book *Compulsion* by Meyer Levin (filmed in 1959 by Richard Fleischer) and Tom Kalin's film *Swoon* (1991) also deal with the same subject.

The Verdict: The way it was filmed has an interesting novelty value, it is well written and played, but it lacks a real spark or edge. 3/5

Under Capricorn (1949)

Cast: Ingrid Bergman (Henrietta Flusky), Joseph Cotten (Sam Flusky), Michael Wilding (Charles Adare), Margaret Leighton (Milly), Jack Watling (Winter), Cecil Parker (Governor), Denis O'Dea (Corrigan)

Crew: Director Alfred Hitchcock, Screenplay James Bridie, Novel Helen Simpson, Producers Sidney Bernstein & Alfred Hitchcock, Original Music Richard Addinsell, Cinematographers Paul Beeson & Jack Cardiff & Ian Craig & Jack Haste & David McNeilly, Film Editing A S Bates

Story: Adare comes to Australia with his relative, the new Governor, and immediately gets acquainted with Flusky, an emancipated prisoner turned shrewd businessman. Being an ex-convict, it is not socially acceptable for Adare to dine with him, so Adare goes. At dinner, Flusky's wife Henrietta makes an appearance, barefooted and drunk. After a scene, where Henrietta sees a monster and Adare pretends to shoot it, we find out the back story. Flusky was a groom who fell in love with Lady Henrietta. They eloped, only for Henrietta's brother to follow them and get shot by Flusky for his trouble. Flusky got seven years transportation and Henrietta followed him. (How did she survive? Prostitution is hinted.) When Flusky got out, they were both different people, but they were obligated to each other and remained together - Flusky built his financial empire, but Henrietta could never be accepted into the polite society she grew up in and found solace in drink. Adare rehabilitates her, even presenting her at the Governor's Ball, but the housekeeper Milly (secretly in love with Flusky) poisons Flusky's mind with talk of Adare and Henrietta. Flusky makes a scene at the ball and in the ensuing argument at Flusky's house, Adare is shot. Flusky is under threat of a second offence and hard labour for life, so Henrietta reveals that she killed her brother and that Flusky did the decent thing by taking the blame for her. Also, Milly had been systematically torturing Henrietta by placing shrunken heads in her bed and encouraging her to drink. In the end, Adare lies in order to clear Flusky of any charges, and to save the woman he loves. Adare is sent home to Ireland, leaving Flusky and Henrietta reunited.

Recurring Ideas: The House (like *Rebecca*); The Wicked Housekeeper (like *Rebecca*); The Man Did Not Murder (like *Rebecca*).

The Walk-On: He appears at the Governor's house, and on the steps of Government House.

The Verdict: A good story, ruined by a bad script, stilted direction and no chemistry between the actors. 2/5

5. On A Roll (1950-1954)

After losing favour with critics and public alike on the self-financed *Rope* and *Under Capricorn*, Hitch tried to gain favour with the bland *Stage Fright*, another financial failure. Thinking, like in 1934, that he should return to what he knew best, Hitch acquired the rights to Patricia Highsmith's novel *Strangers On A Train* and began to build up his reputation again. From then on he made more hits than misses.

Stage Fright (1950)

Cast: Marlene Dietrich (Charlotte Inwood), Jane Wyman (Eve Gill), Richard Todd (Jonathan/Jonny Cooper), Michael Wilding (Inspector Wilfred O Smith), Alastair Sim (Commodore Gill), Sybil Thorndike (Mrs Gill), Kay Walsh (Nellie Goode), Miles Malleson (Bibulous Gent), Joyce Grenfell (Shooting Gallery Attendant), André Morell (Inspector Byard), Patricia Hitchcock (Chubby Banister)

Crew: Director & Producer Alfred Hitchcock, Screenplay Whitfield Cook & Alma Reville, Additional Dialogue James Bridie, Novel Selwyn Jepson, Original Music Leighton Lucas, Cinematographer Wilkie Cooper, Film Editing Emard Jarins

Blonde Virgin: Jane Wyman if she had blonde hair.

The MacGuffin: The bloodstained dress.

Story: Eluding the police in a car, Jonny tells Eve about his affair with Miss Charlotte Inwood, the great theatrical star. Charlotte turned up at his apartment wearing a bloodstained dress. She had killed her husband but needed a clean dress so Jonny went back to get one, messed up the place to make it look like a break-in, was seen and escaped, found Eve at the Royal Academy of Dramatic Art (RADA) and wants her help. Eve is in love with Jonny and takes him to her father's house. While Jonny hides, Eve plays detective to prove his innocence. She meets Inspector Wilfred O Smith, an ordinary, gentle man whom she tries to pump for information, but whom she falls for instead. Eve also becomes Charlotte's dresser, Doris, by paying off the greedy Nellie Goode. After the death of her husband, Charlotte is more concerned about making money in her play - she says Jonny was infatuated with her. Jonny tries to blackmail her with the bloodstained dress. A microphone is secretly set up in the theatre to trap Charlotte, but it turns out that Jonny has killed before and that he is the murderer. Eve realises this when she's alone with him, under the stage.

"She goaded me into doing it. I can't control myself," Jonny says, then looks menacingly at Eve, "If I killed for a third time that'd be a clear case of insanity." Trying to escape, Jonny slips on the stage and is killed by the falling safety curtain.

Visual Ideas: Opens with a safety curtain rising, as in a theatre, and ends with the SAFEty curtain killing the villain. Hitch is still throwing the camera around for some long takes and wordy dialogue, which is to the film's detriment.

Subtext: Theatre (It's about actors, acting roles (Eve plays Doris, Nellie's cousin), about costumes (the bloodstained dress), about make-up (Eve takes make-up OFF to play Doris), about music (Smith plays piano) - at one stage Eve's father says it's like they are all part of a melodramatic play because they have a plot, interesting characters and even a costume).

Recurring Ideas: Wrong Man/Man On The Run (That's Jonny); The Switch (That's Jonny again - he's not the Wrong Man but the villain you know).

The Walk-On: While Jane Wyman is walking along the street, practising her accent as Doris, Hitch walks past and looks back at her, wondering about her curious behaviour.

The Verdict: The flashback is a lie, which I think is great, but Jonny is not a strong villain (he's afraid and strong villains make the best pictures) and no one is in any real danger. The only tension generated is by Eve trying to avoid being found out as Doris, which is pretty weak. 2/5

Strangers On A Train (1951)

Cast: Farley Granger (Guy Haines), Robert Walker (Bruno Antony), Ruth Roman (Anne Morton), Leo G Carroll (Senator Morton), Patricia Hitchcock (Barbara Morton), Marion Lorne (Mrs Antony), Howard St John (Captain Turley), Jonathan Hale (Mr Antony), Robert Gist (Hennessy), Laura Elliot (Miriam Haines)

Crew: Director & Producer Alfred Hitchcock, Screenplay Raymond Chandler & Whitfield Cook & Czenzi Ormonde & Ben Hecht, Novel Patricia Highsmith, Original Music Dimitri Tiomkin, Cinematographer Robert Burks, Film Editing William H Ziegler

Blonde Virgin: Bruno Antony perhaps?

The MacGuffin: Guy's lighter.

Story: Tennis star Guy Haines meets professional layabout Bruno Antony on a train, and Bruno says he's come up with the perfect murder where two people who have never met before swap murders, so there is no apparent motive. (Guy's wife, Miriam, won't give him a divorce and Bruno's rich father won't give him any money.) To humour him, Guy says that it is a good idea and gets off the train. Bruno goes ahead and kills Miriam, then haunts Guy so that Guy will kill Bruno's father. Eventually Bruno resorts to blackmail, saying that he will place Guy's lighter at the place Miriam was killed, framing Guy for the murder. Guy plays tennis at Forrest Lawn while Bruno makes his way to the murder spot, and it is a race against time. Eventually, Bruno and Guy fight on a speeding carrousel, and Bruno is killed when it crashes.

The Source Material: The novel is more concerned about Guy's disintegration after he kills Bruno's father, and Bruno's main motivation is not to kill his father but to live his life with Guy, with whom he imagines an amorous relationship. The gay element is put right into the background of the film - although there is something in Bruno's eyes which indicate it is there.

Visual Ideas: Circles (Balloons, lights, tennis rackets, carrousel, glasses); Parallels (Train tracks, blinds, the bars of the park which look like the bars of a jail); Glasses (Miriam's glasses through which we see her murder. Babara's glasses through which we see a lighter. The blind man Bruno helps across the road after the murder).

Audio Ideas: Silence (This is a very important sound for Hitch, used throughout the murder, so that you can hear every little sound between the silences).

Recurring Ideas: Twins/Doubles (Everything is in twos: two cabs, two pairs of feet, two-tone shoes, two rackets, parallel tracks criss-crossing as two men intersect, Guy playing doubles, cigarette lighter with two rackets, they drink a pair of doubles, later Bruno feels he has been double-crossed, Babara Morton looks like Miriam); Cultured Villain (Bruno's dress sense, his way with older women, his cleanliness, his strangling, suggest Joseph Cotten's Uncle Charlie in *Shadow Of A Doubt*); Public Places (It ends in a fairground, but we also see the Jefferson Memorial and tennis at Forrest Lawn); Trains; The Wrong Man/Hero's Guilt (Guy didn't do it, although he would have liked to. Also he isn't very sympathetic, showing no remorse for Miriam's death and seeming to worry more about his career); Amateur Interested In Murder (Barbara Morton is interested in gory murders); Tiepin (Bruno has a personalised tiepin).

The Walk-On: Hitch is seen boarding a train carrying a Bass violin.

The Verdict: A generally tight plot (with a few holes), horrible people, Robert Walker as a superb villain, dynamic editing, realistic photography. A return to form for Hitch. 4/5

I Confess (1953)

Cast: Montgomery Clift (Father Michael Logan), Anne Baxter (Ruth Grandfort), Karl Malden (Inspector Larrue), Brian Aherne (Willy Robertson), O E Hasse (Otto Keller), Roger Dann (Pierre Grandfort), Charles André (Father Millais), Dolly Haas (Alma Keller), Ovila Légaré (Villette)

Crew: Director & Producer Alfred Hitchcock, Screenplay William Archibald & George Tabori, Play *Our Two Consciences* Paul Anthelme, Associate Producer Barbara Keon, Original Music Dimitri Tiomkin, Cinematographer Robert Burks, Film Editing Rudi Fehr, Technical Advisor Father Paul LaCouline

Blonde Virgin: Anne Baxter.

The MacGuffin: Love.

Story: Villette, a lawyer, is murdered and Keller confesses his crime to Father Logan, who is also his employer. A priest was seen leaving the murder scene and Inspector Larrue suspects Logan. Larrue sees Logan with a mystery woman outside Villette's and tracks her down - she is Ruth Grandfort, the wife of an important politician. Ruth agrees to answer questions to clear Logan because they were together at the time of the murder. Thus it is revealed that Ruth and Logan were once in love, that Logan went off to war and that Ruth married in the meantime. When Logan returned they went out to the countryside, were caught in a storm and stayed in a gazebo overnight, where Villette saw them the next morning and said they had slept together. Logan, who had changed after the war, went into the priesthood and Villette haunted Ruth. Villette began to blackmail Ruth, which is why Ruth and Logan met. Instead of providing Logan with an alibi, Ruth provides him with a motive (he had time to commit the murder) and there is a trial. Everybody considers Logan guilty and Keller even testifies against Logan. Found not guilty, Logan is attacked by the crowd. Keller's wife, Alma, who had planted evidence against Logan, goes into the crowd to tell them Logan is innocent. Keller shoots her and runs to the Château Frontenac, where he reveals Logan is innocent and is shot. Keller asks for forgiveness and Father Logan gives him the last rites. Ruth, realising that Logan loves God more than he loves her, leaves.

Visual Ideas: Opens with shots of Quebec and the Château Frontenac, where the film ends. Over breakfast, we see Alma looking at Father Logan while the other priests talk - this is important because we see what she is thinking (what will Father Logan do?) when they are the only two characters not talking. Hitch uses buildings, faces and walls to divide the screen space so that we can only see part of it.

Audio Ideas: Virtually everybody in this film is referred to by their surnames, which gives it a formal air, as opposed to most of Hitch's other movies where first names are used. Together with the location photography, this gives the film a documentary air.

Recurring Ideas: Shame (Larrue, a man of responsibility, is always right, but he is proved wrong); Public Place (Conclusion at Courthouse & Château Frontenac); Hero's Guilt (Logan would like Villette dead).

The Original Ending: Hitch wanted Father Logan to hang for the crime and then be proved innocent but the studio thought that this would offend religious groups.

The Walk-On: Right at the beginning, Hitch is seen crossing the street at the top of a long staircase.

The Verdict: This is a first-class film, where all the actors are warm except Clift who can only communicate through his eyes since he is given little dialogue. Austere and sober, the film lacks an ironic viewpoint and comes across as flat. There are no points of real tension. 3/5

Dial M For Murder (1954)

Cast: Ray Milland (Tony Wendice), Grace Kelly (Margot Wendice), Robert Cummings (Mark Halliday), John Williams (Inspector Hubbard), Anthony Dawson (Captain Swan/Lesgate)

Crew: Director & Producer Alfred Hitchcock, Screenplay/Play Frederick Knott, Original Music Dimitri Tiomkin, Cinematographer Robert Burks, Film Editing Rudi Fehr

Blonde Virgin: Grace Kelly.

The MacGuffin: A Latchkey.

Story: Tony Wendice knows that his wife Margot had an affair with American mystery writer Mark Halliday in the past. Then Halliday returns to London for a visit. While Mark and Margot are out one night, Tony invites Captain Lesgate to visit on the pretext that Tony wants to purchase an American car from Lesgate. Tony reveals to Lesgate the details of his wife's affair, and then asks Lesgate to kill her, explaining the plan. Lesgate agrees, being a bit of a cad. At the appointed time, while Tony is out with Mark, Tony rings home to make Margot come to the phone, to be near Lesgate. Lesgate is killed by Margot (scissors in his back). Since everything has not gone to plan, when Tony gets back he rearranges the evidence. Based on this evidence, Inspector Hubbard concludes that Margot planned the murder, so she is tried, found guilty and sentenced to death. The day before Margot is executed, Hubbard tricks both Margot and Tony with a key and Tony is revealed to have planned Margot's murder.

Visual Ideas: This was done in 3-D so it's a little difficult to appreciate fully. However, I did notice a lot of shots with a fore, middle and background. Also, many long shots still appear. When Tony is explaining the murder plan to Lesgate, it's all done on a God shot (from very high looking down). Tony playing with the latchkey is very much like Alicia in *Notorious*. The attack on Margot and Lesgate's death are incredibly violent and affecting (especially when Lesgate pulls back Margot by the neck, and when Lesgate, with scissors in his back, falls on his back and, in slow motion, they are forced in further.) When Margot is tried and convicted, we see her face and a coloured background, just like in *Spellbound* when we see Dr Peterson react to Ballantine's conviction.

Recurring Ideas: The Cultured Villain (Tony even offers everybody a drink at the end, after he's caught); Keys (Like in *Notorious*); Impaled - Ouch (Lesgate impaled on scissors, as John Ballantine's brother was impaled in *Spellbound*).

The Walk-On: Hitch is one of the people in the class reunion photo.

The Verdict: Not classic Hitch, but workmanlike. 2/5

6. Auteur Theory (1954-1960)

In the mid-to-late 1950s, Hitch became untouchable. He was a great film-maker, at the height of his powers. The subjects of his films varied, from moneymaking suspense and action, to more risky black comedy, documentary and psychological studies. Also, some film critics started to take more notice of Hitchcock. Although André Bazin, influential French critic and co-founder of *Cahiers Du Cinéma*, said that Hitch was just a technician doing craftsmanlike work, others had a different view. In response to Bazin, French critics and film directors Erich Rohmer and Claude Chabrol joined forces to write the first critical book about Hitch published in 1957. It was to be the first of many such books which put Hitchcock forward as a film-maker with something to say about the human condition.

At the same time as his critical reappraisal, Hitchcock had begun a half-hour television series, *Alfred Hitchcock Presents*, which further promoted Hitch's name and image to the general public, although the bulk of the work was done by Joan Harrison and Norman Lloyd.

Rear Window (1954)

Cast: James Stewart (L B 'Jeff' Jeffries), Grace Kelly (Lisa Carol Fremont), Wendell Corey (Thomas J Doyle), Thelma Ritter (Stella), Raymond Burr (Lars Thorwald), Irene Winston (Mrs Thorwald)

Crew: Director & Producer Alfred Hitchcock, Screenplay John Michael Hayes, Story Cornell Woolrich, Original Music Franz Waxman, Additional Music Friedrich von Flotow (from 'Martha'), Cinematographer Robert Burks, Film Editing George Tomasini

Blonde Virgin: Grace Kelly.

The MacGuffin: The Wedding Ring.

Story: Photographer Jeff is in a wheelchair with a leg in plaster, spending his time looking through his window at the people in the apartments overlooking the courtyard. They are: The Torso, a beautiful dancer with men all around her; Miss Lonelyhearts, the loveless older woman who pretends men visit her; the Newly-weds, who constantly have sex; the childless couple who dote on their dog; the musician who cannot sell his songs; the sculptress; and the salesman with the invalid wife. Jeff and Lisa are in love, but Jeff refuses to marry Lisa because they are not compatible: he travels the world living rough, whilst she is the toast of high society in the latest haute couture. Then, one night, Jeff hears a scream. Later, he sees the salesman leave with his sample case several times during the night. He sees Lars Thorwald, the salesman, wrap up a saw and knives, clean his bathroom, work in his garden and get a trunk picked up. Jeff suspects Thorwald has killed his wife and gets his police friend Doyle to help him. Doyle says Mrs Thorwald is in Meritsville. Seeing Lars with his wife's jewellery, including her wedding ring, totally convinces Lisa and Jeff's nurse Stella that Mrs Thorwald is dead. Also, when the neighbour's dog is killed, everybody comes out to see what the commotion is except Lars. Jeff gets Lars out of his apartment. Lisa and Stella use the time to go into the yard to dig up the garden where the dog was seen rummaging but find nothing, so Lisa goes into Lars' apartment searching for the wedding ring. Lars returns and catches her, they fight, and the police arrive just in time. Lisa, with her hands behind her back, where Jeff can see her, points to the wedding ring on her finger, and Lars sees that Jeff is the one spying on him. While Lisa and Stella are at the police station, Lars attacks Jeff. He is saved by the police, but not before breaking his other leg. In the end, Lisa is out of her dresses and dressed in something more rugged, her daring actions having presumably won her man over.

Visual Ideas: This opens with the window blinds rising, like the safety curtain in *Stage Fright*. The opening roving camera shots (the first of many) introduce all the neighbours and, by touring Jeff's room, reveal him to be an adventurous photographer who got his leg broken by taking a dangerous picture at a motor car race. Being a photographer means that he is naturally curious, and leads him to use binoculars, a camera with a zoom lens, a slide viewer and eventually flashbulbs to blind Lars when he attacks. When Lisa goes to kiss the sleeping Jeff, Hitch shows it in slow motion, giving a delicate sense of intimacy. The multiple windows, with different actions in each, shot at the same time, give the same impression (but to better effect) as split screen techniques which were the vogue in the 1960s (*The Boston Strangler* etc.). When Jeff is writing a note to get Lars out of his apartment, it is a high shot which goes close up so that you can read the note.

Audio Ideas: We hear the musician's song from first faltering notes to full orchestral score. The sounds of day and night in a city are beautifully evoked and realised. Most of the film is without dialogue because of the extended 'silent' stories being told.

Subtext: Believe it or not, this is about love. Each of the neighbours shows a different aspect of love. The Torso is beauty, the newly-weds the joy of sex, Miss Lonelyhearts a lack of love, the salesman and his wife a love gone wrong. They reflect the fears and desires of Jeff, who desires Lisa but fears marrying her. Thorwald and his invalid wife are a dark reflection of invalid Jeff and Lisa. When Lisa does some dangerous things, Jeff looks at her with love in his eyes, because he realises that she has the spirit he's looking for. Lisa goes to Lars' apartment looking for the wedding ring which will convict Lars of murder. When she gets the ring, it's also symbolic of marriage between her and Jeff. When Lisa goes to jail, he gives his camera (his prized possession, his livelihood) for bail, which is symbolic of his love for her.

Recurring Ideas: Doubles (The Thorwalds and Jeff/Lisa); The Screen (Jeff's window is a screen, which allows us to see all the other screens/ windows, each of which tells a story. It is only at the end that the villain looks back through Jeff's window); Birds (There are caged birds); Egg (Jeff cannot eat his eggs when Stella talks about murder).

The Walk-On: Hitch is seen winding a clock in the musician's apartment.

The Verdict: Pure cinema, great dialogue and storytelling, fascinating from the first moment, this rates as one of Hitch's best. 5/5

To Catch A Thief (1955)

Cast: Cary Grant (John Robie), Grace Kelly (Frances Stevens), Jessie Royce Landis (Jessie Stevens), John Williams (H H Hughson), Charles Vanel (Bertani), Brigitte Auber (Danielle Foussard), Jean Martinelli (Foussard), Georgette Anys (Germaine)

Crew: Director & Producer Alfred Hitchcock, Screenplay John Michael Hayes, Novel David Dodge, Original Music Lyn Murray, Cinematographer Robert Burks, Film Editing George Tomasini

Blonde Virgin: Grace Kelly/Brigitte Auber.

The MacGuffin: The Cat.

Story: A series of jewel thefts on the South coast of France leads the police to suspect John Robie, known as The Cat, who retired 15 years previously after he and his fellow prisoners fought with the Resistance during World War Two and gained parole. While being chased by the police, Robie must prove his innocence by catching the new Cat. Robie makes contact with his old Resistance friends to hide him but they despise him for turning crook again. Danielle the daughter of one of his old Resistance friends helps him escape, and pursues him romantically. He links up with insurance man Hughson, who gives Robie a list of the people with the most valuable jewels, and Robie decides to link up with American oil-millionairess Jessie Stevens and her daughter Frances. Frances pursues Robie romantically and, with Jessie and Hughson, decides to catch the new Cat at a costume ball where everybody will be bringing their jewels. After a rooftop chase The Cat turns out to be Danielle, and Robie ends up with Frances, a girl who doesn't wear jewels.

Visual Ideas: Begins with a woman screaming with an open mouth. The burglar, called The Cat, is represented by a cat prowling the rooftops, and then we cut to a black cat in Robie's house. At points of unease while Robie is with Bertani, Hitch uses high shots of Robie to make him small, and low shots of Bertani to make him big. When Robie and Frances consummate their courtship, the flurry of fireworks represent the sexual act.

Audio Ideas: This must have more sexual puns and doubles entendres than any of Hitch's other movies.

Recurring Ideas: The Wrong Man/Man On The Run; Birds (Caged birds on the bus); Egg (Jessie stubs her cigarette in the yoke of an egg); The Scream; Cats (Robie has nine lives, Hughson picks tails on the toss of a coin, Danielle and Frances are catty when they talk, Robie walks catlike, someone offers him a saucer of milk); The Double (Hughson pretends to be Robie at the costume ball).

The Walk-On: Hitch is on a bus, beside Cary Grant.

And Another Thing: Robert Burks rightfully won an Oscar for his sumptuous cinematography.

The Verdict: A delightful concoction, as light as French pastry. 3/5

The Trouble With Harry (1955)

Cast: Edmund Gwenn (Captain Albert Wiles), John Forsythe (Sam Marlowe), Mildred Natwick (Miss Gravely), Mildred Dunnock (Mrs Wiggs), Jerry Mathers (Arnie Rogers), Royal Dano (Calvin Wiggs), Parker Fennelly (Millionaire), Barry Macollum (Tramp), Dwight Marfield (Dr Greenbow), Shirley MacLaine (Jennifer Rogers), Leslie Wolff (Art Critic), Philip Truex (Harry Worp)

Crew: Director & Producer Alfred Hitchcock, Screenplay John Michael Hayes, Novel Jack Trevor Story, Associate Producer Herbert Coleman, Original Music Bernard Herrmann, Cinematographer Robert Burks, Film Editing Alma Macrorie

Blonde Virgin: Shirley MacLaine, although she has dark hair, a boy and has been married twice.

The MacGuffin: Harry.

Story: A small boy with a toy gun is walking in the woods when he comes across a dead body, so he runs back to tell his mum. In the meantime the ageing Captain Wiles, who was out shooting rabbits, believes he has killed the man - Harry Worp - by accident. Before he can bury him, spinster Miss Gravely, Arnie and his young mother Jennifer Rogers, a tramp, Dr Greenbow and artist Sam Marlow all come across the body. It turns out Jennifer was married to Worp and is glad he's dead. The tramp takes the dead man's shoes. Sam draws a portrait of Harry. And Miss Gravely is not surprised by the body (believing herself to have killed him in a struggle). Over the course of a day Harry is buried and exhumed four times by Captain Wiles, Sam, Jennifer and Miss Gravely. When they discover that Harry died of a heart attack, they put him back where they found him and have Arnie discover the body all over again. Oh, Sam falls in love with Jennifer, and Captain Wiles falls for Miss Gravely.

Visual Ideas: It's beautifully photographed, highlighting the reds and oranges of the Autumn foliage. There are very few trick shots.

The Walk-On: Hitch is at an outdoor art exhibition.

The Verdict: A light, whimsical piece of nonsense that fails to raise much interest. 2/5

The Man Who Knew Too Much (1956)

Cast: James Stewart (Doctor Ben McKenna), Doris Day (Jo McKenna), Brenda De Banzie (Mrs Drayton), Bernard Miles (Mr Drayton), Ralph Truman (Buchanan), Daniel Gélin (Louis Bernard), Mogens Wieth (Ambassador), Alan Mowbray (Val Parnell), Hillary Brooke (Jan Peterson), Christopher Olsen (Hank McKenna), Reggie Nalder (The Assassin), Betty Bascomb (Edna), Bernard Herrmann (Himself, as conductor)

Crew: Director & Producer Alfred Hitchcock, Screenplay John Michael Hayes, Story Charles Bennett & D B Wyndham-Lewis, Associate Producer Herbert Coleman, Original Music Bernard Herrmann, Songs Ray Evans & Jay Livingston, Cinematographer Robert Burks, Film Editing George Tomasini

Blonde Virgin: Doris Day.

The MacGuffin: The Assassination.

Story: Dr Ben and Jo McKenna are vacationing in Marrakech with their son when they witness the assassination of a secret agent, who tells them of a plot to kill a foreign Prime Minister in London. Their son is kidnapped by a spy ring, led by Mr Drayton, to ensure their silence. The couple go to London to track down the kidnappers, and Jo cries out during the concert at the Albert Hall, thus preventing the assassination. At the Prime Minister's Embassy, Jo sings (she used to be a famous singer) while Ben searches the Embassy for their son. As Mr Drayton holds them hostage, Ben pushes Drayton down the stairs - whilst falling Drayton shoots himself.

Visual Ideas: There is a well-handled police chase through the market at Marrakech. Ben's face is in darkness when he hears his son is held hostage. In London, when Ben and Jo receive a phone call at the airport, they are seen embracing from a high shot, showing their need for each other and that they are small and alone. In contrast to Marrakech, where there are lots of people, in London tension is created by there being no people around at all. At the Albert Hall, too many things happen to adequately condense here, but it's very tense, with people and guns slowly moving into position (it's mostly done in slow motion now). At the Embassy, we 'see' Jo's singing travel through the corridors by shots of empty staircases and the song becoming weaker/hollower, until it comes through the keyhole of the room where Hank is imprisoned.

Audio Ideas: The credits have the music which ends in the cymbals crashing. The spies listen to the music on record several times, agreeing that the shot will be on the clash of the cymbals. Then we get the music in the Albert Hall, now waiting for the shot as the cymbals clash. At Ambrose Chapel, Jo has to sing badly, otherwise she'll stand out from the crowd. When Ben rings Ambrose Chappell to talk about his son, there are lots of people around, so tension is caused by Ben not being able to talk freely.

Recurring Ideas: The Cultured Villain (Drayton seemed like such a nice man); The Switch (Louis Bernard is seen as sinister at the beginning but becomes good when he is assassinated. Mrs Drayton switches sides when she finds out the boy is to be killed); The Tower (Towers in Marrakech, bell tower in London); Public Places (Marrakech Market, Ambrose Chapel, Albert Hall, Embassy).

The Walk-On: In the Marrakech market, Hitch is seen watching the acrobats, although you need to see it in widescreen to spot him.

The Verdict: Despite interesting ideas, and some good suspense moments in Ambrose Chapel and at the Albert Hall, it takes a long time to get going. Also, the death of the villain is weak (as is the villain himself).
3/5

The Wrong Man (1956)

Cast: Henry Fonda (Manny Balestrero), Vera Miles (Rose Balestrero), Anthony Quayle (Frank O'Connor), Harold Stone (Lt. Bowers)

Crew: Director & Producer Alfred Hitchcock, Screenplay Maxwell Anderson & Angus MacPhail, Book *The True Story Of Christopher Emmanuel Balestrero* Maxwell Anderson, Associate Producer Herbert Coleman, Original Music Bernard Herrmann, Cinematographer Robert Burks, Film Editing George Tomasini, Technical Advisors George Groves & Frank D O'Connor

Blonde Virgin: Vera Miles.

The MacGuffin: Justice.

Story: Manny is a musician at The Stork Club. When he goes to an insurance office to take out a loan on his wife's insurance, the women there identify him as the man who held up the office twice before. Manny is arrested, interviewed, identified in a line-up, paraded in front of store owners, booked, held overnight, arraigned and put in jail. His family raises bail and hires lawyer O'Connor to represent him. However, the strain of the ordeal is too much for Manny's wife, Rose, and she must be put in a mental institution. The trial begins and the witnesses once again identify Manny as the hold-up man. When a juror complains about O'Connor's questions a mistrial is ruled, so the process must begin all over again. Manny prays for a miracle and, as he does so, the real hold-up man is caught robbing a store. After Manny is acquitted, he visits Rose to give her the good news, but her mind will take years to heal, if it ever does.

Visual Ideas: Stark black & white realism is the style - amazingly real photography, yet with the Hitchcock touches we know and love: following Manny through his door; seeing the police station and jail through Manny's eyes; seeing half a face; Manny looking at hands and feet of his fellow prisoners, not their faces; Rose seen as small or at angles to show that she is retreating from the world; the bad people (the police) shown in a menacing top light. Like *Rear Window*, this is a model of storytelling since most of Manny's emotions are transmitted through pictures, not words.

Audio Ideas: Manny's growing terror of the process of being booked is shown by both his face, and by the growing noise of the process, culminating in the jail where lots and lots of prisoners can be heard but none of them seen (because Manny is alone). The ironic dialogue - at the beginning, Manny says to Rose that they are lucky people, and they also talk of the millions of years of evolution which have brought them here.

Subtext: Hitchcock was always keen to show the true cost of people's actions, and usually presented his thesis within the framework of melo-drama. In this case, it is not some symbolic villain, a reincarnation of fate, who picks The Wrong Man out of a hat and does bad things to him. In this case, it is the System of Justice which is the villain - not only does it phys-ically incarcerate Manny, but it mentally traps Rose's mind. Her doctor describes her as being in "a maze of terror," "a frightening world" and that she can't "get out of the nightmare."

Recurring Ideas: The Wrong Man (Obviously); The Double (Manny is the physical double for the hold-up man. Rose is in a nightmare world of her own as Manny is in the nightmarish world of reality); Process/The Cultured Villain/The Family Of Villains (The due process of law is the villain of this story. It is polite, clean and well dressed. There is also a family of processes all working together: the police, the District Attorney, the courts, the jails).

And Another Thing: Hitch used the same buildings, the same words and, in some cases, the same people involved in the case.

The Walk-On: Hitch is in the diner.

The Verdict: Although told like a documentary this is full of Hitch-cock's usual themes and touches. Another classic. 5/5

Vertigo (1958)

Cast: James Stewart (John 'Scottie' Ferguson), Kim Novak (Madeleine Elster/Judy Barton), Barbara Bel Geddes (Marjorie 'Midge' Wood), Tom Helmore (Gavin Elster)

Crew: Director & Producer Alfred Hitchcock, Screenplay Samuel A Taylor & Alec Coppel, Novel *The Living And The Dead* Pierre Boileau & Thomas Narcejac, Associate Producer Herbert Coleman, Original Music Bernard Herrmann, Cinematographer Robert Burks, Film Editing George Tomasini, Title Designer Saul Bass

Blonde Virgin: Kim Novak/Barbara Bel Geddes.

The MacGuffin: Love.

Story: Detective Scottie is chasing a criminal across the rooftops of San Francisco when he discovers he has vertigo - a fear of heights - and causes the death of a policeman. Recovering and retired - he has independent means - he relaxes with his best friend Midge, a college friend who loves him, although Scottie doesn't realise it. Another old college friend, Gavin

Elster, wants Scottie to follow his wife Madeleine because he believes her to be possessed by the spirit of her grandmother, Carlotta Valdez, who committed suicide. Scottie follows Madeleine, and falls in love with her. When she throws herself into the bay, he saves her. They love each other, but Madeleine is compelled to go to a church tower, where she falls and dies. Scottie is heartbroken - his vertigo stopped him from saving her - and his mind becomes unhinged and he goes to a mental hospital. Midge helps him recover, but she knows Scottie still loves Madeleine. Released, everything and everyone Scottie sees remind him of Her, and then he sees her double, Judy Barton. Following her, he begins to change her into the Madeleine he wants. (We know that she is the same woman, that she was used by Elster to imitate his wife, that Elster knew Scottie had vertigo, and that it was Elster's wife who fell from the tower, not Judy. Also, we know that Judy fell in love with Scottie for real. It is only a matter of time before Scottie finds this out.) When Judy wears Carlotta Valdez's necklace, Scottie knows that Madeleine and Judy are the same person and takes her back to the church tower. In his anger, he forces her to the top, overcoming his vertigo and, as they profess their love for each other, Judy cowers away from a shadow and falls to her death, leaving Scottie wrought with guilt and woe.

Visual Ideas: Where to begin? When Scottie meets Elster, the framing is symmetrical, their body language is the same then changes as they talk, Scottie starting high (in power position) and Elster low, and ending up reversed as Scottie is persuaded by Elster's argument. At Ernie's restaurant, we pan from Scottie to the room, the music kicks in, and we track in slowly to Madeleine: she is wearing green, and is seen from the side (aloof). Madeleine is seen in mirrors several times, as is Judy. It is all about dressing and undressing (Scottie undresses Madeleine when he saves her from the Bay, and then proceeds to dress Judy as Madeleine - the undressing allowed him to be precise in this matter). The first half is seen from Scottie's point of view, and the second from Judy's.

Subtext: The key to this extraordinary work is the visit to the Sequoias. We see a cross-section of an old tree trunk, and history is shown repeating itself through wars and treaties. And the name of the trees translates as "Always green, everlasting." This explains why, when we first see Madeleine, and then later Judy Barton, she is wearing green and in profile. Madeleine even drives a green car. Also, the green light (from the neon light) bathes Judy when she is transformed back into Madeleine. Carlotta becomes Madeleine becomes Judy - they are objects of love reincarnated, remade, over and over. They are everlasting, because Scottie will always love her, even after death. It's a romantic, gothic idea played out in bright sunshine.

Recurring Ideas: Doubles (Madeleine Elster thinks she's Carlotta Valdes but she's really Judy Barton. Judy makes the crack that Scottie can't kiss her because she's got her face on. Midge paints herself as Carlotta Valdes. Scottie kills two people through his vertigo, and the love of his life dies twice); The Cultured Villain (Gavin Elster is Scottie's school friend, owner of a shipbuilding business); Towers (The tower at the mission).

The Walk-On: Hitch walks by the entrance of the shipbuilding yard carrying a bugle case. He sure does a lot of walking for a man of his girth.

And Another Thing: Since filming *Rebecca*, Hitch had been searching for a way to capture the sensation of falling, and he discovered it in *Vertigo*. The camera focuses on a fixed point, then moves away from that fixed point while at the same time zooming in. When done correctly, you get the elongation effect seen in *Vertigo*. This shot is now a standard tool in the industry, usually used to show strangeness or alienation at an appropriate moment.

The Verdict: Simply a classic. Wordless for most of its length, it says more as a result. The film gains resonance from repeated viewing. 5/5

North By Northwest (1959)

Cast: Cary Grant (Roger Thornhill), Eva Marie Saint (Eve Kendall), James Mason (Phillip Vandamm), Jessie Royce Landis (Clara Thornhill), Leo G Carroll (The Professor), Philip Ober (Lester Townsend), Martin Landau (Leonard), Adam Williams (Valerian), Edward Platt (Victor Larrabee), Robert Ellenstein (Licht)

Crew: Director & Producer Alfred Hitchcock, Screenplay Ernest Lehman, Associate Producer Herbert Coleman, Original Music Bernard Herrmann, Cinematographer Robert Burks, Film Editing George Tomasini, Title Designer Saul Bass

Blonde Virgin: Eva Marie Saint.

The MacGuffin: Microfilm in a statue.

Story: Advertising executive Roger Thornhill is mistaken for George Kaplan, and taken to a big house, owned by Mr Townsend, where he is questioned. When he fails to come up with any answers, he is forced to drink a bottle of bourbon, put in a stolen car and pointed in the direction of a cliff. Thornhill gains control of the car and is arrested by the police. His story is checked out, but everything is normal and nobody believes him.

Thornhill tracks Townsend down in the United Nations building, only it's not the Townsend he talked to. Townsend is killed with a knife in his back, Thornhill is photographed with the knife in his hand and becomes a man on the run. We find out Kaplan is an imaginary spy set up by the FBI to deflect suspicion away from their inside agent. On a train to Chicago, Thornhill meets beautiful Eve Kendall and they make love, only Eve is working for Vandamm (the fake Townsend). They set a trap. Thornhill is in the middle of nowhere, waiting to meet Kaplan, but he is attacked by a plane. Escaping, Thornhill is angry with Eve, and goads her and Vandamm at an auction. Trapped by Vandamm's men all around, Thornhill causes trouble so that he's arrested. The police release him to The Professor of the FBI, they fly North by Northwest airlines to Mount Rushmore — Eve is an FBI spy and she is in danger because of what Thornhill said at the auction. Eve shoots Thornhill to regain the confidence of Vandamm — shoots with blanks. Thornhill tries to stop Eve leaving the country with Vandamm and the microfilm (in the statue Vandamm bought at the auction) and saves her life, only to be pursued onto the face of Mount Rushmore. After a struggle, Eve and Thornhill live to get married.

Visual Ideas: There are many little touches, but the one truly outstanding sequence is the crop-dusting plane attacking Thornhill. After so many scenes of noisy cities and trains, the quiet in the middle of nowhere is deafening. Thornhill looks in all directions, but it is empty - no Kaplan. Cars pass. Then we hear the drone of a plane in the far distance. A car emerges from the fields and deposits a man - Kaplan? Thornhill talks to him, but he's not the one. When the stranger gets on his bus, the plane attacks like some angry bee.

Recurring Ideas: The Wrong Man/Man On The Run; The Train; The Cultured Villain (When caught, and henchman Leonard is shot, Vandamm says, "That isn't terribly sporting - using real bullets"); The Public Place (UN, Train station, Auction, Café, Mount Rushmore); The Switch (Eve is helpful, then an enemy spy, then a friendly spy, then a wife); Clenched Hands (When he's angry with Eve, Thornhill clenches his hands); Overbearing Mother.

The Walk-On: Just after the credits, Hitch runs to catch a bus but the door slams in his face.

And Another Thing: Jessie Royce Landis, who plays Thornhill's mother, was actually a year younger than Cary Grant.

The Verdict: The last word in the lighthearted chase romp before more serious/pompous/comic copies came along like the Bond thrillers. 5/5

Psycho (1960)

Cast: Anthony Perkins (Norman Bates), Vera Miles (Lila Crane), John Gavin (Sam Loomis), Martin Balsam (Milton Arbogast), John McIntire (Sheriff Chambers), Lurene Tuttle (Mrs Chambers), Patricia Hitchcock (Caroline), Janet Leigh (Marion Crane), Virginia Gregg & Paul Jasmin & Jeanette Nolan (Voice of Mother)

Crew: Director & Producer Alfred Hitchcock, Screenplay Joseph Stefano, Novel Robert Bloch, Original Music Bernard Herrmann, Cinematographer John L Russell, Film Editing George Tomasini, Pictorial Consultant & Title Designer Saul Bass

Blonde Virgin: Marion Crane.

The MacGuffin: $40,000.

Story: Marion Crane steals $40,000 from her boss at the real estate office in Phoenix, Arizona, and heads for her lover Sam Loomis in Fairvale, California. Tired, she stops at the Bates Motel. After talking to Norman, she decides to go home and return the money but before doing that she is attacked and killed in the shower by Mrs Bates. Norman painstakingly cleans up and disposes of the body and car (and, unknowingly, of the $40,000). The following week, Sam Loomis is visited by Marion's sister Lila and a private detective, Milton Arbogast, who is looking for the money on behalf of Marion's employer. Arbogast visits all the local hotels, talks to Norman and, eventually, finds out Marion was there. He tells Lila about this, then returns to talk to frail old Mrs Bates. As Arbogast is walking up the stairs, Mrs Bates kills him. While Lila and Sam look for Arbogast, Norman carries the frail Mrs Bates down to the cellar. Pretending to be a couple, Sam keeps Norman talking while Lila searches the house - she finds the decaying corpse of Mrs Bates, and is attacked by Norman in a dress and wig. Norman has a split personality. He shares his mind with his mother, but now his mother has taken over forever.

Visual Ideas: The shower scene and Arbogast's murder are the two amazing set pieces. When Arbogast is interviewing Norman, there is a brilliant shot of Norman's head stretched over, looking like one of the birds he stuffs.

Subtext: When Marion (a sexual, strong creature) talks to Norman (a timid, weak creature), they get quite close, close enough for Norman to change Marion's mind. "I think we're all in our own private traps," Norman says, "We all go a little mad sometimes." So Norman, to some extent, is aware of his own problems, although we are never allowed to sympathise with him or see things from his point of view. Some of his dialogue is ironic: "My mother isn't quite herself today", "I don't hate her, I hate what she has become, the illness", "A boy's best friend is his mother." Otherwise, Norman just leers.

Recurring Ideas: Overbearing Mother (That Mrs Bates - she's a nasty piece of work if you ask me); The Double (Norman has two sides of his personality, also Marion and Lila Crane look like one another); Birds (Norman stuffs birds and looks like one himself, and Crane is a bird); Hands; Process (The detailed procedure for cleaning up Marion Crane's blood); The Switch (The movie starts as a crime film and changes to a horror movie).

The Walk-On: Bizarrely, Hitch is seen standing outside the real-estate office wearing a ten-gallon hat.

And Another Thing: Norman was based on the real-life murderer Ed Gein, whose crimes were far too horrific to be included here. The movie spawned a couple of sequels 20 years later, and thousands of imitators almost immediately.

The Verdict: A daring premise (follow the woman and the money, then kill the woman and lose the money, then start another story), boldly executed. 5/5

7. Beyond The Frame (1963-1976)

Hitch's movies were a series of situations linked together by plot. They were not character driven. This meant that Hitch relied on major stars to carry the emotion of the story. From the early 1960s, Hitch was without Cary Grant and James Stewart, and most of the famous actors were from the emerging Method school who wanted the character's development to be the central focus. In addition, Hitch was losing control of his performers. He would develop a project around a big star, then the star would drop out for one reason or another. Without a star to follow, Hitch was lost, so he tried to invent his own in Tippi Hedren. The experiment failed. After that, Hitch lurched from one thing to another, seemingly without purpose or interest. Unsure of his vision and his script, Hitch began to improvise on the set of *The Birds* and his later films. Hitch lost confidence. The only high point in this later period was *Frenzy*, filmed in his native London.

The Birds (1963)

Cast: Rod Taylor (Mitch Brenner), Jessica Tandy (Lydia Brenner), Suzanne Pleshette (Annie Hayworth), Tippi Hedren (Melanie Daniels), Veronica Cartwright (Cathy Brenner), Ethel Griffies (Mrs Bundy), Charles McGraw (Sebastian Sholes), Ruth McDevitt (Mrs MacGruder), Lonny Chapman (Deke Carter)

Crew: Director & Producer Alfred Hitchcock, Screenplay Evan Hunter, Story Daphne Du Maurier, Cinematographer Robert Burks, Film Editing George Tomasini, Electronic Sound Effects Bernard Herrmann & Oskar Sala

Blonde Virgin: Tippi Hedren.

The MacGuffin: Peace of mind.

Story: Lawyer Mitch Brenner meets rich girl Melanie Daniels in a pet shop and treats her like a shop assistant. He is playing a joke on her since he once tried to prosecute her in court for a practical joke that went wrong. They argue, and Melanie tries to get her own back by presenting Mitch's little sister with the two Lovebirds Mitch couldn't find in the pet shop. She has to travel from San Francisco to Bodega Bay. After secretly delivering the present, Melanie is attacked by a seagull. As Melanie is introduced to Mitch's family (Cathy loves her, Mitch's mother Lydia is afraid Mitch will leave her - like when her husband died) and schoolteacher Annie Hayworth (she loves Mitch, they once had a relationship, she moved to

Bodega Bay to be near him), the different species of birds escalate their attack: gulls attack Cathy's outdoor birthday party; sparrows fill the house by coming down the chimney; Lydia finds a dead farmer with his eyes gouged out; crows attack the schoolchildren; gulls attack the town which goes up in flames; and Annie is killed saving Cathy. Mitch, Melanie, Lydia and Cathy board themselves up in the house, only to have the birds attack but not get in. Melanie, having shown courage, is now loved by Mitch and accepted by Lydia. During the night, Melanie investigates a sound and is trapped in the loft, repeatedly pecked by an onslaught of birds. Dragged out by Mitch, she is in shock. Mitch goes outside and all the buildings and land are covered with birds. They tiptoe out, and slowly make their way by car to some uncertain future.

Visual Ideas: Broken Crockery (When the sparrows attack, they break all the crockery in the house, which upsets Lydia. When Lydia visits the farmer to talk about chicken grain, she knows something is wrong because she sees broken cups); One Too Many (When Melanie sits outside the school, we see the crows slowly amassing on the climbing frame behind her. She is agitated, smoking. Then she sees a crow, follows its flight and then it lands on the climbing frame where there are hundreds of crows); Glass (The attacks are seen through the restaurant window, a telephone booth and a car window, but then the birds begin smashing through the glass as well); God Shot (When the town goes up in flames and there is much action, Hitch cuts to a high shot of the whole town, has one bird swoop and hover close to us, and then another, and another, until the screen is filled with birds).

Audio Ideas: There is no music in this film, only natural and unnatural sounds. The sound of the birds massing is frightening.

Recurring Ideas: Birds (We start in a pet shop full of caged birds, Melanie brings Lovebirds for Cathy, the chickens won't eat grain, chicken is served at the restaurant, and obviously there are many bird attacks); Interest In Murder (Cathy is interested in murders); The Double (Have a look at Lydia and Melanie - they look similar); Hats (Mitch catches the escaped bird in the pet shop with his hat).

The Walk-On: Near the beginning Hitch is leaving the pet shop with two Scottie dogs.

The Verdict: Garden birds turning against mankind shows how the banal can become terrifying. One day, everything changes and you have to live with it whether you like it or not. Accept the situation: we have nuclear power, cold war, a new member in of the family. 4/5

Marnie (1964)

Cast: Tippi Hedren (Marnie Edgar), Sean Connery (Mark Rutland), Diane Baker (Lil Mainwaring), Martin Gabel (Sidney Strutt), Louise Latham (Bernice Edgar, Marnie's mother), Bob Sweeney (Cousin Bob), Mariette Hartley (Susan Clabon), Alan Napier (Mr Rutland), Bruce Dern (Sailor), Melody Thomas Scott (Young Marnie)

Crew: Director & Producer Alfred Hitchcock, Screenplay Jay Presson Allen, Novel Winston Graham, Original Music Bernard Herrmann, Cinematographer Robert Burks, Film Editing George Tomasini

Blonde Virgin: Tippi Hedren.

The MacGuffin: Sex.

Story: Marnie gets into a position of responsibility at a company, steals money from their safe, then disappears, rides her horse, then changes identity and does it all over again. She begins work for Mark Rutland, who recognises her from one of her previous places of employment. He falls in love with her, rumbles her scheme and forces her to marry him. On their honeymoon he finds out she is repulsed by the idea of men touching her and having sex. Eventually, he rapes her. When they return home, Mark tries to find out why Marnie is frigid and he uses his background knowledge (he used to study predators, the "criminals of the animal world") and his money to find out about Marnie's mind and past. After an accident forces Marnie to kill her horse (the only thing she likes between her legs), she tries to steal Mark's money. He catches her, brings Marnie to her mother in Baltimore and the truth is revealed - as a child Marnie helped kill a sailor who was visiting her mother, a prostitute.

Visual Ideas: Instead of lines in white in *Spellbound*, the colour red on white is the trigger that upsets Marnie. The scene where she steals money from Rutland's office is great. At the party, there is a pan from the top of the stairs, down, through the guests and close up on the face of Strutt, that recalls previous Hitch films but does not have the emotional power because it has not been set up properly.

Recurring Ideas: Double (Marnie is several people); Overbearing Mother (Marnie's mother is horrible to her); *Spellbound* (There is a dream to interpret, a trigger (red on white) and Marnie is cured by reliving the bad experience (killing the sailor)).

The Walk-On: Hitch is seen leaving a hotel room.

The Verdict: The psychology harks back to *Spellbound*, another one that didn't work, and the two main actors are terribly miscast (Connery says "old bean" all the time, Hedren just goes through the motions). 2/5

Torn Curtain (1966)

Cast: Paul Newman (Professor Michael Armstrong), Julie Andrews (Sarah Sherman), Lila Kedrova (Countess Luchinska), Hansjörg Felmy (Heinrich Gerhard), Tamara Toumanova (Ballerina), Wolfgang Kieling (Hermann Gromek), Ludwig Donath (Professor Gustav Lindt), Günter Strack (Professor Karl Manfred), David Opatoshu (Jakobi), Gisela Fischer (Dr Koska), Mort Mills (Farmer), Carolyn Conwell (Farmer's Wife)

Crew: Director & Producer Alfred Hitchcock, Screenplay Brian Moore, Original Music John Addison, Cinematographer John F Warren, Film Editing Bud Hoffman

Blonde Virgin: Julie Andrews.

The MacGuffin: A formula in Professor Lindt's head.

Story: Professor Michael Armstrong (physicist) and Sarah Sherman (assistant) are in bed, in love and engaged to be married. Sarah knows something is wrong and follows Michael - he defects to East Germany. Michael wants to get a formula out of Professor Lindt's head and goads him into giving it. Realising that Michael is not a traitor, Sarah does everything she can to help. Once Michael has the formula, they must escape back to the West.

Visual Ideas: There is one stunning scene in this film, in the farmhouse, when Michael and the farmer's wife kill Michael's bodyguard Gromek. It is not as easy to kill someone as one might suppose, and Hitch shows each idea as it enters the woman's head. Gun? No, the taxi driver is outside and he would hear the noise. Knife? Michael and Gromek are rotating and swaying too quickly to be accurate. When the knife is in Gromek, it snaps off. Next, a spade is applied to Gromek's legs - we see how much it hurts by cuts to his face reacting. When Gromek falls to the floor, he is still alive, grasping Armstrong by the neck. The woman opens the oven, turns on the gas, they slowly drag Gromek to it, put his head in and, in a high shot looking down, we see Gromek's hands flail about, twitch and stop. With the spade the farmer's wife indicates that she will bury both Gromek and his motorbike.

Recurring Ideas: On The Run; Birds (Gromek, who speaks amusingly in American slang, even when he is dying, says, "Strictly for the boirds"); Hands (Michael looks at his bloodstained hands, then washes them); Silent Dialogue (Michael tells Sarah the truth in a long shot as Karl looks on but we don't hear what he says, just as in *North By Northwest* Thornhill and The Professor explain everything to each other and we only hear the plane's engine); Stairs (We see straight down circular stairs and all the hands on the rails); Screens (Standing in front of a bank of television screens); Public Place (Theatre, University, Post Office).

The Walk-On: When Hitch's TV show theme is played, he's seen in the hotel lobby with a baby on his lap.

The Verdict: This is not a bad film but it makes a serious error. At the beginning, the emotional dynamics between Sarah and Michael are excellently handled and tension is created by their changing circumstances. However, halfway through, as they realise they are both on the same side and in love with each other, the emotional tension is dissipated and it becomes one long get-out-of-the-country chase. 3/5

Topaz (1969)

Cast: Frederick Stafford (André Devereaux), Dany Robin (Nicole Devereaux), Karin Dor (Juanita de Cordoba), John Vernon (Rico Parra), Claude Jade (Michèle Picard), Michel Subor (François Picard), Michel Piccoli (Jacques Granville), Philippe Noiret (Henri Jarre), John Forsythe (Michael Nordstrom), Roscoe Lee Browne (Philippe Dubois), Per-Axel Arosenius (Boris Kusenov), Sonja Kolthoff (Mrs Kusenov), Tina Hedström (Tamara Kusenov)

Crew: Director & Producer Alfred Hitchcock, Screenplay Samuel A Taylor, Novel Leon Uris, Associate Producer Herbert Coleman, Original Music Maurice Jarre, Cinematographer Jack Hildyard, Film Editing William H Ziegler

Blonde Virgin: Dany Robin.

The MacGuffin: A ring of spies.

Story: It's 1962 and everybody is worried about whether or not there are missiles in Cuba. When Boris Kusenov defects to the US, he says the Cubans have missiles. As a favour to the Americans, French spy André Devereaux first goes to New York to steal information from Cuban Ambassador Rico Parra, then goes to Cuba and gets confirmation. His contact in Cuba, and lover, Juanita de Cordoba is killed by Parra. Back in Paris, it's obvious that French Intelligence have a ring of Soviet spies in their midst, called 'Topaz,' so Devereaux uses his family to draw them out. The ringleader, Jacques Granville, kills himself when he is discovered.

Visual Ideas: Like the opening of *Blackmail*, the first shot of the Soviet Embassy in Copenhagen tracks from high up, down and into a face in a mirror. A close-up of tortured spies tracks out to a large jail space, harking back to a similar shot in *Murder!* A high shot looks down as Parra shoots

Juanita and, as she falls, her skirt opens like a flower, like blood. We look down the middle of a spiral staircase. At the high-level meeting we are close up to the people as they enter and track back to reveal an enormous, ornate room as it fills, and then track back in to a close-up of Granville as he is told to go away.

Recurring Ideas: Process (We see figurines being made in Copenhagen); The Cultured Villain (Jacques Granville beds Mrs Devereaux, and he's French!); Public Place (Kusenov and family defect/are picked up outside a department store); Silent Talk (Devereaux talks to Dubois behind a glass door in the flower shop. Dubois talks to Uribe in the hotel lobby); Birds (Gulls carrying the hollowed-out bread used to transport a camera are seen by guards, thus alerting them to the spies - and no I'm not making this up to see if you are still reading).

The Wheel-On: At the airport, Hitch is in a wheelchair, attended by a nurse when he gets up to shake someone's hand.

The Verdict: This is the equivalent of listening to the concert of a great singer about a mile from the stadium – it is only a glimpse of greatness. Remarkable only for getting made in the first place. 1/5

Frenzy (1972)

Cast: Jon Finch (Richard Blaney), Alec McCowen (Inspector Oxford), Barry Foster (Bob Rusk), Billie Whitelaw (Hettie Porter), Barbara Leigh-Hunt (Brenda Blaney), Vivien Merchant (Mrs Oxford), Anna Massey (Barbara 'Babs' Milligan), Bernard Cribbins (Felix Forsythe), Michael Bates (Sergeant Spearman), Jean Marsh (Monica Barling, Brenda's secretary)

Crew: Director & Producer Alfred Hitchcock, Screenplay Anthony Shaffer, Novel *Goodbye Piccadilly, Farewell Leicester Square* Arthur La Bern, Associate Producer William Hill, Original Music Ron Goodwin, Cinematographers Leonard J South & Gilbert Taylor, Film Editing John Jympson

Blonde Virgin: Barbara Leigh-Hunt.

The MacGuffin: Sating your desires.

Story: In London, women are strangled with neckties and, when Brenda Blaney is killed in the office of her dating agency, suspicion falls on her ex-husband, the unsympathetic lout and ex-Squadron Leader Richard Blaney. The murderer is his friend, mummy's boy and likeable Covent Garden grocer Bob Rusk, who has "certain peculiarities" when it comes to women. Inspector Oxford is assigned the case. Blaney goes on the run, is helped by girlfriend Babs and hides out at the Porters'. When Babs goes to pick up her clothes, she's met by Rusk ("Remember, Bob's your uncle") and killed. Rusk puts her body in a potato bag and then onto a truck. When he returns home, Rusk realises his tiepin is missing so goes back to the truck, but the truck starts on its journey North with Rusk in the back trying to pry his tiepin from Babs' dead fingers. He gets off at a truck stop. When Blaney turns up at Rusk's for help, Rusk takes him in and hands him over to the police - Blaney now knows Rusk is the killer and vows to kill him. Whilst serving life in prison, Blaney throws himself down the stairs, is put into hospital and escapes. Sneaking into Rusk's room, Blaney smashes an iron bar into the head of the sleeper, only to find it's a murdered girl. Inspector Oxford enters, waits and Rusk enters with a trunk. Oxford says, "Mr Rusk, you're not wearing your tie."

Visual Ideas: A smooth helicopter shot down the Thames over the credits. When Rusk picks up Babs, we have a tracking shot up his stairs - then it's completely quiet, we go back down the stairs and out to Covent Garden, the sound growing. When Blaney escapes hospital, there's a high shot showing him blend in with the doctors and then make his way out.

Audio Ideas: We hear Blaney's trial as snatches of sound when a guard opens and closes the door, anxious to hear the verdict - otherwise it is silent.

Recurring Ideas: The Wrong Man/Man On The Run; The Cultured Villain; The Smart-Aleck Crowd (When the body washes up on the shore of the Thames, the crowd makes cracks about the latest necktie murder, "I say, that isn't my club tie, is it?"); Food (Set in Covent Garden. Rusk is a grocer. He eats an apple whilst killing Brenda Blaney. He puts Babs on a potato truck. Inspector Oxford is plagued by a wife who makes exotic meals).

The Watch-On: Hitch, wearing a bowler hat, is in the crowd engrossed by the dead body.

The Verdict: This has echoes of the London of *The Lodger*, although it is more explicit in its handling of rape and murder. Also, we have a horrible hero, who is somehow more believable because of his awful behaviour. A brilliant return to form. 4/5

Family Plot (1976)

Cast: Karen Black (Fran), Bruce Dern (George Lumley), Barbara Harris (Blanche Tyler), William Devane (Arthur Adamson), Ed Lauter (Joseph Maloney), Cathleen Nesbitt (Julia Rainbird), Katherine Helmond (Mrs Maloney)

Crew: Director & Producer Alfred Hitchcock, Screenplay Ernest Lehman, Novel *The Rainbird Pattern* Victor Canning, Original Music John Williams, Cinematographer Leonard J South, Film Editing J Terry Williams

Blonde Virgin: Barbara Harris.

The MacGuffin: Eddie Shoebridge.

Story: Psychic Blanche Tyler and her boyfriend/actor/cab driver George Lumley are trying to track down Eddie Shoebridge, the illegitimate child of the late Harriet Rainbird and heir to a fortune, so that they can collect a $10,000 finder's fee. Simultaneously, Arthur Adamson and Fran kidnap an important person and ask for a diamond as ransom. As George finds out more information and a bishop is kidnapped during a mass, it becomes apparent that Eddie Shoebridge and Arthur Adamson are one and the same. After Arthur's friend Maloney tries and fails to kill Blanche and George, Blanche finds Arthur and is kidnapped for her trouble. George follows, they capture Arthur and Fran, and find the diamond in a chandelier.

Visual Ideas: After George brakes suddenly for a woman crossing the road, we pan with her walking across the road and up to a guard on a gate. In Arthur's house, the chandelier (where the diamond is hidden) is in the foreground when panning up and down the stairs. At her husband's funeral, Mrs Maloney kicks over Eddie Shoebridge's headstone.

Recurring Ideas: The Cultured Villain (He's a respectable jeweller); The Switch (Fran is happy to kidnap, but will not kill); Public Place (The bishop is kidnapped during mass); Theatre (Arthur and Fran dress up as a priest and old woman); Birds (The expression "A bird in the hand" is used); Crystal (As well as a crystal ball being seen in the credit sequence, George says, "You have me by the crystal balls," we see the diamonds sparkle and the chandelier is full of crystal glass).

The Weight-On: Hitch is seen in silhouette behind the door of the department of vital statistics.

The Verdict: An enjoyable, lightweight movie. 3/5

The Short Night

Having completed *Family Plot*, Hitch worked on *The Short Night*, a script based on the British spy George Blake, who escaped from prison and was helped out of the country by gangland London. The screenplay begins with an action sequence (the escape from prison & England), has a middle section about the Blake character's wife in Finland having an affair with the counter-espionage agent after him, and then the final action sequence where the Blake character commandeers a train to get over the Russian border. Hitch's failing health (2 pacemaker operations) and his having to look after Alma (she had a stroke) meant he couldn't physically film on location. Hitch shut up shop. He was feted by the American Film Institute when he received their Life Achievement Award in 1979. Everybody he worked with was there but Hitch was in a wheelchair and looked quite ill. Attendees feared the worse but, to everybody's surprise, he got up and gave a witty and charming speech. He was knighted in the New Year's Honours list for 1980. Then, while in hospital, he died peacefully in his sleep on the morning of 29 April 1980.

Reference Materials

Books

Alfred Hitchcock And The Making Of Psycho by Stephen Rebello, UK: Marion Boyars Publishers, 1998, Paperback, 224 pages, £12.95, ISBN 0714530034. *Psycho* is a great movie, but somehow Stephen Rebello manages to flatten it out and fashion it into a boring shape. Beginning with chapters on mass murderer Ed Gein and novelist Robert Bloch, we then move onto the well-researched chapters on the production itself. Rebello spends too much time being nice to everybody by recounting their different memories of the same event, giving the whole thing a static feel. Also, unlike other biographers, he gives Saul Bass a lot of credit for the shower scene and other sequences in the movie. It's easy to read, and reveals how different scenes were filmed, added and cut, but I wasn't excited by it.

Alfred Hitchcock's Rear Window by John Belton, Cambridge University Press, 1999, £10.95, ISBN 0521564530.

Blackmail by Tom Ryall, UK: BFI Publishing, 1994, Paperback, 64 pages, £7.99, ISBN 0851703569. *Blackmail* is generally acknowledged to be the first British talkie. Generally acknowledged, but not quite accurate since Tom Ryall points out that *The Clew Of The New Pin* was released in March 1929, five months before Hitchcock's film. So, although not the first British talkie, it was certainly the first British talkie to make a lasting impression. Tom Ryall has taken a research approach to the book, breaking it down into sections on the development of sound film, British International Pictures who produced *Blackmail*, the making of the film, the critical reception and finally a shot-by-shot analysis. This is a short book (55 pages of text), and the amount of words devoted to general tangential matters points to the lack of information available on this film. The 'making of' section is a mere 4 pages, yet Ryall devotes 11 pages to a history of critical writing about Hitchcock. A short read, short on information about Hitchcock and his work, yet it is filled with (excruciating) details about the history of sound in British films.

Hitch: The Life And Times Of Alfred Hitchcock by John Russell Taylor, UK: Abacus, 1981, Paperback, 304 pages, £2.75, ISBN 0349133859, US: Da Capo Press, 1996, Paperback, 336 pages, $14.95, ISBN 0306806770. The authorised biography, which means that a lot of material in the Truffaut book also appears here (although with more background detail) and, as you might expect, it shows Hitch in a good light. The best thing about it is the insight it gives to Hitch's relationship with his wife Alma.

Hitchcock by François Truffaut & Helen G Scott, UK: Paladin, 1986, Paperback, 574 pages, £8.95, ISBN 0586086536, US: Touchstone Press, 1985, Paperback, 367 pages, $21.00, ISBN 0671604295. Easily the most interesting and easy to read book on Hitchcock, this is one long interview with the master, conducted by film director/critic Truffaut, translated by Scott. Hitch talks about each film up until *Torn Curtain*, and then Truffaut writes about the last remaining movies, using correspondence and other mini-interviews. Profusely illustrated and informative, it does suffer occasionally from Hitch mis-remembering bits from his films - something I only discovered through actually watching them. Despite this small criticism, this is *The Bible* for Hitchcock fans.

Hitchcock On Hitchcock: Selected Writings And Interviews by Alfred Hitchcock, ed Sidney Gottlieb, UK: Faber And Faber, 1997, Paperback, 360 pages, £11.99, ISBN 0571191363, US: University Of California Press, 1997, Paperback, 360 pages, $16.95, ISBN 0520212223. Although Hitch is well known for his interviews, he also wrote extensively about the cinema. Many of his articles, together with short interviews, are gathered together in this book. Not essential to the Hitch collection, but a lot of fun.

Hitchcock Poster Art by Mark H Wolff & Tony Nourmand, Aurum Press, August 1999, Paperback, 128 pages, £14.99, ISBN 1854106430. Here is something for the dedicated Hitchcock fan - rare Hitchcock posters and lobby cards from around the world. Superbly reproduced and selected, there are genuine rarities here, including the only known copy of the American *Woman To Woman* poster, a film on which Hitch was assistant director. Notice that *Saboteur* (1942) is the first poster to have Hitchcock's name above the title. Although Hitch's photo appears on the poster for *Juno And The Paycock* (1930), his black humour persona is not used until *Rope* (1948). Marvel at the brilliantly designed Polish posters which all feature skulls - *The Birds* is a skull with wings, *Stage Fright* is a skull drawn from the black squares of a crossword grid.

Hitchcock: The First Forty-Four Films by Eric Rohmer & Claude Chabrol, UK: Roundhouse Publishing, 1992, Paperback, 188 pages, £6.95, ISBN 1857100069. Originally published in 1957, this was the first book to recognise Hitchcock as a director worth serious consideration.

Hitchcock's America ed Jonathan Freedman & Richard Millington, UK: Oxford University Press, 1999, Hardcover, 224 pages, £30.00, ISBN 0195119053, US: Oxford University Press USA, 1999, Hardcover, 224 pages, $24.00, ISBN 0195119061. This is a collection of scholarly essays about how Hitchcock portrayed American culture in his movies. There are some good ideas in it, but it's difficult to get at them because the book is written by academics for academics, so every second word mentions postmodernism or some philosopher nobody else has ever heard of. I've given my copy away.

Hitchcock's Films Revisited by Robin Wood, Columbia University Press, 1990, Paperback, $22.00, ISBN 0231065515.

Hitchcock's Secret Notebooks by Dan Auiler, Bloomsbury, 1999, Hardcover, 576 pages, £20.00, ISBN 0747544905.

Me And Hitch by Evan Hunter, Faber And Faber, Paperback, 91 pages, £3.99, ISBN 0571193064. Evan Hunter, who writes crime novels as Ed McBain, wrote the screenplay for *The Birds* and the first draft of *Marnie*. Here, in captivating prose, he recounts his daily meetings with Hitch.

North By Northwest by Ernest Lehman, UK: Faber And Faber, 1999, Paperback, 144 pages, £8.99, ISBN 0571201849. The screenplay of Alfred Hitchcock's romantic thriller, written by the screenwriter of *Sweet Smell Of Success* and *The Sound Of Music*.

The Alfred Hitchcock Story by Ken Mogg, Titan Books, 1999, Hardcover, 192 pages, £29.99, ISBN 1840230916. Although this tome is full of insight, the approach is so reverential that it lacks critical objectivity. However, this shrine to Hitchcock is lavishly illustrated with rare behind-the-scenes photos, which makes it an essential purchase.

The Birds by Camille Paglia, UK: BFI Publishing, 1998, Paperback, 80 pages, £7.99, ISBN 0851706517. This is proof, if proof is needed, that the BFI's Film Classics series is occasionally capable of brilliance. Camille Paglia is well known for having forceful and forthright opinions. This book is no exception. Presented initially as a reminiscence of her original viewing of the film, it turns into a detailed examination of the plot, smartly and incisively interjected with precise research, with penetrating diversions into the subtext. Reading this book, it felt as though I was watching a lot of the film for the first time. This freshness is truly invigorating, and I would highly recommend it.

The Complete Hitchcock by Paul Condon & Jim Sangster, Virgin Publishing, 1999, Paperback, 224 pages, £14.99, ISBN 075350362X. Imagine a book with a similar layout to this, but much longer and with different opinions, and you have *The Complete Hitchcock*. Replete with many references to modern films, and sometimes with slightly more trivia that we need to know, it is nevertheless an informative starter pack for Hitchcock's films. It contains very little information about Hitch and his life, since the authors are primarily interested in the films.

The Dark Side Of Genius - The Life Of Alfred Hitchcock by Donald Spoto, UK: Plexus Publishing, Paperback, 608 pages, £12.99, ISBN 0859652130. This biography takes a critical look at Hitch, turning him into some sort of sadistic monster in the process. Spoto sees Hitch's desire to be in control of everything to do with his productions, especially his leading ladies, as a bad thing. Tippi Hedren is generally used as an example but, as far as I can see, Hitch had every right to change Hedren, a model who couldn't act, who was plucked out of obscurity by Hitch to worldwide publicity. Spoto's biography is bigger, has more research and gives a better idea of critical and public response to Hitch. Despite its bias, it is an essential read.

The Rebecca Project by Lauren Rabinovitz & Greg Easley, BFI Publishing, CD-ROM, £40.00, ISBN 0813521513. This multimedia CD-ROM contains Quick Time movie clips, photographs, hypertext critical essays and rarely seen primary documents.

Vertigo: The Making Of A Hitchcock Classic by Dan Auiler, UK: Titan Books, 1999, Hardcover, 231 pages, £19.99, ISBN 1840230657, US: St Martin's Press, 1998, Hardcover, 231 pages, $27.95, ISBN 0312169159.

Hitchcock On The Web

The Definitive Hitchcock Links Page - http://www.geocities.com/Hollywood/Cinema/2434/hitchlinks.htm - As the name might suggest, start here for days of fun surfing the web in search of Hitchcock trivia courtesy of John Courke.

The MacGuffin Web Page - www.labryinth.net.au/~muffin/ - An online version of *The MacGuffin Journal*, a magazine devoted to Hitch and his work. Edited by Ken Mogg, it's a very scholarly approach, which is sometimes off-putting, but once you get used to it, a brilliant resource.

The Master Of Suspense - www.geocities.com/SunsetStrip/Towers/7260/hitch.html - For information on the Hitchcock TV shows, as well as some of the more esoteric aspects of Hitch's films, visit Patrik Wikström's site.

Advertising Hitchcock - www.geocities.com/Hollywood/Cinema/2434/ - Like to see a lot of Hitch's film posters? Visit Martin Dawber's fascinating site.

The Essential Library: Currently Available

Film Directors:

Woody Allen (Revised)	Tim Burton	Ang Lee
Jane Campion (£2.99)	John Carpenter	Steve Soderbergh
Jackie Chan	Joel & Ethan Coen	Clint Eastwood
David Cronenberg	Terry Gilliam (£2.99)	
Alfred Hitchcock	Krzysztof Kieslowski (£2.99)	
Stanley Kubrick	Sergio Leone	
David Lynch	Brian De Palma (£2.99)	
Sam Peckinpah (£2.99)	Ridley Scott	
Orson Welles	Billy Wilder	
Steven Spielberg	Mike Hodges	

Film Genres:

Film Noir	Hong Kong Heroic Bloodshed (£2.99)
Horror Films	Slasher Movies
Spaghetti Westerns	Vampire Films (£2.99)
Blaxploitation Films	Bollywood
French New Wave	

Film Subjects:

Laurel & Hardy	Marx Brothers
Steve McQueen (£2.99)	Marilyn Monroe
The Oscars®	Filming On A Microbudget
Bruce Lee	Film Music

TV:

Doctor Who

Literature:

Cyberpunk	Philip K Dick
Agatha Christie	Noir Fiction (£2.99)
Terry Pratchett	Sherlock Holmes
Hitchhiker's Guide	Alan Moore

Ideas:

Conspiracy Theories	Nietzsche
Feminism	Freud & Psychoanalysis

History:

Alchemy & Alchemists	The Crusades
American Civil War	American Indian Wars
The Black Death	Jack The Ripper
The Rise Of New Labour	Ancient Greece

Available at all good bookstores or send a cheque (payable to 'Oldcastle Books') to: **Pocket Essentials (Dept AH2), 18 Coleswood Rd, Harpenden, Herts, AL5 1EQ, UK.** £3.99 each unless otherwise stated. For each book add 50p postage & packing in the UK and £1 elsewhere.